Workshop on Narrative Understanding (WNU 2019)

Minneapolis, Minnesota, USA
7 June 2019

ISBN: 978-1-5108-8778-7

Printed from e-media with permission by:

Curran Associates, Inc.
57 Morehouse Lane
Red Hook, NY 12571

Some format issues inherent in the e-media version may also appear in this print version.

Printed by Curran Associates, Inc. (2019)

Association for Computational Linguistics
209 N. Eighth Street
Stroudsburg, Pennsylvania 18360

Phone: 1-570-476-8006
Fax: 1-570-476-0860

acl@aclweb.org

Additional copies of this publication are available from:

Curran Associates, Inc.
57 Morehouse Lane
Red Hook, NY 12571 USA
Phone: 845-758-0400
Fax: 845-758-2633
Email: curran@proceedings.com
Web: www.proceedings.com

NAACL HLT 2019

Workshop on Narrative Understanding (WNU)

Proceedings of the First Workshop

June 7, 2019 Minneapolis, Minnesota

Introduction

Welcome to the first Workshop on Narrative Understanding!

This interdisciplinary workshop aims to bring together researchers from natural language processing, machine learning, and other computational fields with humanities scholars to discuss methods to improve and evaluate automatic narrative understanding capabilities.

In addition to papers on a variety of topics (including non-archival submissions that do not appear in this proceedings but will be presented at the workshop), we are excited to host invited talks by Nanyung Peng, Mark Riedl and Richard So.

We would like to thank all submitters and program committee members, and hope that you enjoy the workshop!

David, Elizabeth, Madalina, Mohit and Snigdha

Organizers:

David Bamman, University of California, Berkeley
Snigdha Chaturvedi, University of California, Santa Cruz
Elizabeth Clark, University of Washington
Madalina Fiterau, University of Massachusetts, Amherst
Mohit Iyyer, University of Massachusetts, Amherst

Program Committee:

Antoine Bosselut, University of Washington
Faeze Brahman, University of California, Santa Cruz
Jan Buys, University of Washington
Lucie Flekova, Amazon Research
Saadia Gabriel, University of Washington
Ryan Heuser, Stanford University
Ari Holtzman, University of Washington
Daphne Ippolito, University of Pennsylvania
Yangfeng Ji, University of Virginia
Rik Koncel-Kedziorski, University of Washington
Lara Martin, Georgia Tech
Nasrin Mostafazadeh, Elemental Cognition
Brendan O'Connor, University of Massachusetts Amherst
Karl Pichotta, University of Texas at Austin
Jonathan Reeve, Columbia University
Melissa Roemmele, SDL Research
Maarten Sap, University of Washington
Matt Sims, University of California, Berkeley
Shashank Srivastava, Carnegie Mellon University/Microsoft Research
Ted Underwood, University of Illinois, Urbana-Champaign

Table of Contents

Conference Program

Friday, June 7, 2019

9:00–9:10 ***Welcome***

9:10–9:50 *Invited talk: "Computational Narratology and Critical Race Theory"*
Richard So

9:50–10:30 *Invited talk*
Nanyun Peng

10:30–11:00 ***Coffee break***

11:00–12:15 **Talks by authors of selected papers**

11:00–11:25 *Towards Coherent and Cohesive Long-form Text Generation*
Woon Sang Cho, Pengchuan Zhang, Yizhe Zhang, Xiujun Li, Michel Galley, Chris Brockett, Mengdi Wang and Jianfeng Gao

11:25–11:50 *Character Identification Refined: A Proposal*
Labiba Jahan and Mark Finlayson

11:50–12:15 *Diverging Paths in Birth Stories: A Medical Dataset for Narrative Analysis*
Maria Antoniak and David Mimno

12:15–12:31 Two-minute madness

12:15–12:17 *Casting Light on Invisible Cities: Computationally Engaging with Literary Criticism*
Shufan Wang and Mohit Iyyer

12:17–12:19 *Deep Natural Language Understanding of News Text*
Jaya Shree, Emily Liu, Andrew Gordon and Jerry Hobbs

12:19–12:21 *Contextualized Word Embeddings Enhanced Event Temporal Relation Extraction for Story Understanding*
Rujun Han, Mengyue Liang, Bashar Alhafni and Nanyun Peng

12:21–12:23 *Extraction of Message Sequence Charts from Narrative History Text*
Girish Palshikar, Sachin Pawar, Sangameshwar Patil, Swapnil Hingmire, Nitin Ramrakhiyani, Harsimran Bedi, Pushpak Bhattacharyya and Vasudeva Varma

12:23–12:25 *Computational Prediction of Elapsed Narrative Time*
Gregory Yauney, Ted Underwood and David Mimno

12:25–12:27 *Unsupervised Hierarchical Story Infilling*
Daphne Ippolito, David Grangier, Chris Callison-Burch and Douglas Eck

12:27–12:29 *Identifying Sensible Lexical Relations in Generated Stories*
Melissa Roemmele

12:29–12:31 *Automatic Story Generation With Human-in-the-Loop*
Faeze Brahman, Alexandru Petrusca and Snigdha Chaturvedi

12:31–14:00 ***Lunch***

14:00–15:30 ***Poster session***

15:30–16:00 ***Coffee break***

Friday, June 7, 2019 (continued)

16:00–16:40 *Invited talk: "Computational Narrative Intelligence and the Quest for the Great Automatic Grammatizator"*
Mark Riedl

16:40–17:00 ***Wrap up / closing remarks***

Towards coherent and cohesive long-form text generation

Woon Sang Cho[⋆] **Pengchuan Zhang**[†] **Yizhe Zhang**[†] **Xiujun Li**[†]
Michel Galley[†] **Chris Brockett**[†] **Mengdi Wang**[⋆] **Jianfeng Gao**[†]
[⋆]Princeton University
[†]Microsoft Research AI
[⋆]{woonsang,mengdiw}@princeton.edu
[†]{penzhan,yizzhang,xiul,mgalley,chrisbkt,jfgao}@microsoft.com

Abstract

Generating coherent and cohesive long-form texts is a challenging task. Previous works relied on large amounts of human-generated texts to train neural language models. However, few attempted to explicitly improve neural language models from the perspectives of coherence and cohesion. In this work, we propose a new neural language model that is equipped with two neural discriminators which provide feedback signals at the levels of sentence (cohesion) and paragraph (coherence). Our model is trained using a simple yet efficient variant of policy gradient, called *negative-critical sequence training*, which is proposed to eliminate the need of training a separate critic for estimating *baseline*. Results demonstrate the effectiveness of our approach, showing improvements over the strong baseline – recurrent attention-based bidirectional MLE-trained neural language model.

1 Introduction

The terms *coherence* and *cohesion* in linguistics are commonly defined as follows (Williams and Colomb, 1995).

- *Cohesion*: sentence pairs fitting together the way two pieces of a jigsaw puzzle do.
- *Coherence*: what all the sentences in a piece of writing add up to, the way all the pieces in a puzzle add up to the picture on the box.

In layman's terms, *cohesion* indicates that two consecutive sentences are *locally* well-connected, and *coherence* indicates that multiple sentences *globally* hold together.

Generating cohesive and coherent natural language texts that span multiple sentences is a challenging task for two principal reasons. First, there is no formal specification of cross-sentence linguistic properties, such as coherence and cohesion of a text. Secondly, there is no widely accepted model to measure the two properties.

Most state-of-the-art neural approaches to natural language generation rely on a large amount of human-generated text to train language models (Cho et al., 2014; Graves, 2013; Sutskever et al., 2014). Although these models can generate sentences that, if judged individually, are similar to human-generated ones, they often fail to capture the local and global dependencies among sentences, resulting in a text that is neither coherent nor cohesive. For example, neural language models based on Recurrent Neural Networks (RNNs) are widely applied to response generation for dialogue (Vinyals and Le, 2015; Shang et al., 2015; Sordoni et al., 2015; Li et al., 2015). Although the responses by themselves look reasonable, they are detached from the whole dialogue session. See Gao et al. (2018) for a comprehensive survey.

In this paper, we address the challenge in a principled manner, employing a pair of discriminators to score whether and to what extent a text is coherent or cohesive. The coherence discriminator measures the compatibility among all sentences in a paragraph. The cohesion discriminator measures the compatibility of each pair of consecutive sentences. These models, given a conditional input text and multiple candidate output texts, are learned to score the candidates with respect to the criterion. The scores are used as reward signals to train an RNN-based language model to generate (more) coherent and cohesive texts.

Contributions. Our main contributions are: (**1**) we propose two neural discriminators for modeling coherence and cohesion of a text for long-form text generation; (**2**) we present a simple yet effective training mechanism to encode these linguistic properties; (**3**) we propose *negative-critical sequence training*, a policy gradient method that uses negative samples to estimate its reward *baseline* and therefore eliminates the need for a sepa-

Proceedings of the First Workshop on Narrative Understanding, pages 1–11
Minneapolis, Minnesota, June 7, 2019.

rate critic function; and (**4**) we develop a new neural language model that generates more coherent and cohesive long-form texts, and empirically validate its effectiveness using the TripAdvisor and Yelp English reviews datasets.

2 Related work

Coherence and cohesion. Coherence and cohesion have been extensively studied in the computational linguistics community, particularly in the 'pre-deep-learning' era. Lack of formal specifications for coherence and cohesion (Mani et al., 1998), resulted in many different formalisms, such as Rhetorical Structure Theory (Mann and Thompson, 1988), and other forms of coherence and cohesion relations and their quantification (Mani et al., 1998; Hobbs, 1985; Hovy, 1988; McKeown, 1985; Cohen and Levesque, 1985; Hovy, 1991; Cristea et al., 1998; Halliday and Hasan, 1996; Liddy, 1991; Van Dijk, 2013; Edmundson, 1969; Barzilay and Lapata, 2008). This list is not exhaustive. However, prior work jointly exploring coherence and cohesion using neural models in the context of long-form text generation has not come to our attention.

Reinforcement learning for text generation. The text generation task can be framed as a reinforcement learning (RL) problem (Daumé et al., 2009), in which the generator G is acting as a *policy* π, with parameters θ_π, and each generated word at time t, w_t, can be viewed as an action to be chosen by the policy from a large discrete space, or vocabulary, conditioned on state $s_{t-1} = w_{\leq t-1}$.

Let r_t be the reward for a partially generated text sequence $w_{\leq t}$. We define the long-term expected reward $\mathcal{J}(\pi) = \mathbb{E}_{s_0 \sim q, \pi}[\sum_{t=1}^{\infty} \gamma^{t-1} r_t]$, where q is the initial distribution of conditional input texts. Following Sutton et al. (1999), the gradient of $\mathcal{J}$ with respect to θ_π is

$$\nabla_{\theta_\pi} \mathcal{J} = \mathbb{E}_{s \sim \rho^\pi, a \sim \pi(\cdot|s)}[Q^\pi(s,a) \nabla_{\theta_\pi} \log \pi_{\theta_\pi}(a|s)]$$

where ρ^π is the stationary distribution and $Q^\pi(s,a)$ is the expected return from state s and taking action a, both following policy π. For brevity, we omit the derivation. In this work, we formulate text generation as an episodic RL problem with episode length L, rewards r_L being available only at the end of episode and $\gamma = 1$.

There are many works on training neural language models using rewards, such as Ranzato et al. (2015) and Paulus et al. (2017). These works directly optimize for specific metrics, such as BLEU (Papineni et al., 2002) or ROUGE (Lin and Hovy, 2003), using REINFORCE (Williams, 1992). However, these metrics do not give a complete picture of the text generation quality. Only recently have there been efforts to provide more relevant objectives, such as consistency and repetition in a text (Li et al., 2015, 2016a; Holtzman et al., 2018). But these works use the objectives to re-rank candidate outputs, not to reward or penalize them. Li et al. (2016b) constructed a set of reward models for the dialogue task, such as information flow and semantic coherence, to tune the generator, yet they do not provide an ablation study on the relative contribution of these reward models individually. It is not clear that these reward models can be generalized to other tasks, in particular, long-form text generation tasks.

The most relevant to our work is Bosselut et al. (2018), which promotes text generation in the correct order, and discourages in its reverse order using rewards. However, this may not be sufficient in capturing coherence since there are many negative orderings given a paragraph. From this pool, we assess the relative quality of generations. Furthermore, we model cohesion between consecutive sentence pairs using word-level features.

GANs for text generation. Another line of research involves the use of Generative Adversarial Networks (GANs) (Goodfellow et al., 2014) to incorporate feedback signals for text generation (Yu et al., 2017; Lin et al., 2017; Zhang et al., 2017; Guo et al., 2017; Fedus et al., 2018; Zhang et al., 2018). The discriminators in these works are trained to distinguish real texts from generated ones, operating as a black-box than providing feedback on linguistic aspects. Yang et al. (2018) partially addressed this issue by using a trained language model as the discriminator. Although the discriminator provides a fine-grained feedback at the word level, it does not model linguistic properties, such as cohesion and coherence.

Many text generator models are inadequate for generating a cohesive and coherent long-form text that span multiple sentences. As a result, human readers can easily distinguish the generated texts from real ones. In this paper, we argue that the primary reason is the lack of an effective mechanism to measure and control for the local and global consistency in model-generated texts.

3 Coherence and Cohesion Models

We assume that global coherence of a text depends to a large degree upon how its individual sentences with different meanings are organized. Therefore, we focus our evaluation of coherence solely based on the sentence-level features. If the sentences are not organized properly, the intention of the paragraph as a whole is obscure, regardless of seamless local connectivity between consecutive sentences.

This is not to say that local connections between any two neighboring sentences can be overlooked. One can easily distinguish a generated sentence from a real one by judging whether it is *semantically cohesive* with its neighboring sentences.

We strive to embody these two different yet important concepts by developing coherence and cohesion discriminators, operating on the sentence level and word level, respectively. Our design of these two discriminators is inspired by the Deep Structured Semantic Model (DSSM) which was originally developed to measure the semantic similarity between two texts (Huang et al., 2013; Gao et al., 2014; Palangi et al., 2016; Xu et al., 2017). In this study, we extend 'semantic similarity' to coherence and cohesion in a long-form text.

3.1 Coherence discriminator: $D_{\text{coherence}}$

The coherence discriminator models the coherence score, which measures how likely two text chunks add up to a single coherent paragraph. Let $S := [s_1, s_2, ..., s_n]$ be the source text chunk that consists of n sentences, $T := [t_1, t_2, ..., t_m]$ be the *real* target text chunk that consists of m sentences, and $\widetilde{T} := [\widetilde{t}_1, \widetilde{t}_2, ..., \widetilde{t}_{\widetilde{m}}]$ be the *artificially constructed incoherent* target text chunk that consists of $\widetilde{m}$ sentences. $D_{\text{coherence}}$ is designed to distinguish a positive (coherent) pair (S, T) from a negative (incoherent) pair $(S, \widetilde{T})$ by assigning different scores, i.e., $D_{\text{coherence}}(S, T) > D_{\text{coherence}}(S, \widetilde{T})$.

Model architecture. The model takes a form of dual encoder. Given source text chunk S and target text chunk T, the coherence discriminator $D_{\text{coherence}}$ computes the coherence score in three steps, as illustrated in Figure 1 (upper). First, each sentence is encoded by the bag-of-words (BOW) embedding, i.e., the average of its word vectors from a pre-trained word embedding (Pennington et al., 2014). Secondly, an encoder which can be implemented using a convolutional neural network

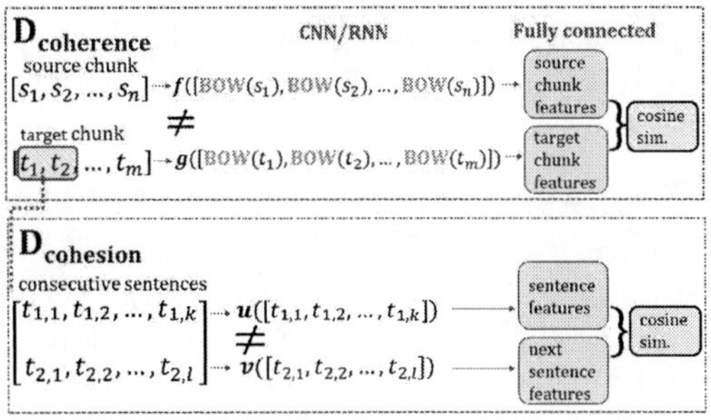

Figure 1: Illustration of coherence and cohesion discriminators. $D_{\text{coherence}}$ takes in bag-of-words sentence embeddings as inputs, and D_{cohesion} takes in the raw word embeddings of consecutive sentences as inputs. The source encoder f (or u) is different from the target encoder g (or v).

(CNN)[1] or RNN[2], denoted as f, takes as input the BOW vectors of the source text chunk S and encodes it into a single vector $f(S)$. Similarly, g encodes the target text chunk T into $g(T)$. The two encoders $f(\cdot)$ and $g(\cdot)$ share the same architecture but do *not* share parameters, i.e., $\theta_f \neq \theta_g$, and thus $D_{\text{coherence}}(S, T)$ is *not* symmetric. Thirdly, $D_{\text{coherence}}(S, T)$ is computed as the cosine similarity of the two vectors $f(S)$ and $g(T)$. The score is a real value between -1 and 1, where 1 indicates maximal coherence, and -1 minimal coherence.

Note that we use the simple BOW vectors to encode sentences in the coherence discriminator, which is different from the CNN sentence embedding scheme in the cohesion discriminator that we introduce in Section 3.2. Although the BOW vector ignores the word-order information in the sentence, it is empirically shown to be effective in preserving the high-level semantic information in the sentences and achieves success in sentence similarity and entailment tasks (Wieting et al., 2016; Arora et al., 2017). Because high-level semantic information of sentences is sufficient to determine whether a paragraph is coherent, we choose to use BOW vectors to encode sentences in $D_{\text{coherence}}$.

The parameters of $D_{\text{coherence}}$, θ_f and θ_g are optimized using a pairwise ranking loss. To this end, we need both positive and negative pairs. While the positive (coherent) pairs come from the train-

[1]We explored with deeper networks. However, the performance difference was marginal. For simplicity, we decided to use a 1-layer convolutional network architecture (Kim, 2014; Collobert et al., 2011).

[2]For clarity in our model description, we omit RNN hereafter. We present results using both CNN and RNN encoders in Table 2.

ing data, negative (incoherent) pairs need to be artificially constructed. The next section describes the way these negative pairs are generated.

Constructing negative (incoherent) pairs. Given a training minibatch $\{(S_i, T_i)\}_{i=1}^B$, we construct $2*B-1$ negative pairs $\{(S_i, \widetilde{T_{i,j}})\}_{j=1}^{2B-1}$ for *every* positive pair (S_i, T_i) using three different methods, inspired by Wieting et al. (2016). For notation simplicity, we omit the minibatch index i in the rest of this section. For each positive pair (S, T) in the minibatch:

- We rotate T with S fixed, and thus obtain all $B-1$ mismatched pairs $\{(S, \widetilde{T}_j)\}_{j=1}^{B-1}$ as negative pairs.
- We shuffle the sentence order in T once, known as a derangement, to break its coherence. This yields one negative pair $(S, \widetilde{T})$.
- We combine the previous two methods, that is, we rotate T in the minibatch and shuffle sentences within the target chunk, yielding another $B-1$ negative pairs $\{(S, \widetilde{T}_j)\}_{j=1}^{B-1}$.

These $2B-1$ negative pairs and a single positive pair, in total, pose a challenge for the discriminator in learning to retrieve the correct pair.

Training using a pairwise ranking loss. The parameters of $f(\cdot)$ and $g(\cdot)$ are optimized in such a way that a positive pair scores higher than its negative pairs, i.e., $D_{\text{coherence}}(S, T) > D_{\text{coherence}}(S, \widetilde{T}_j)$ for any j. To achieve this, we propose to minimize the following pairwise ranking loss (Gong et al., 2013) with margin δ:

$$L_{\text{coherence}}(\theta_f, \theta_g) := \max\Big(0, \delta - D_{\text{coherence}}(S, T) + \text{AVG}^{\lambda}\Big(\{D_{\text{coherence}}(S, \widetilde{T}_j)\}_{j=1}^{2B-1}\Big)\Big). \quad (1)$$

where $\text{AVG}^{\lambda}(\{x_j\}_{j=1}^N) = \sum_{j=1}^N w_j x_j$ and $w_j = e^{\lambda x_j} / \sum_k e^{\lambda x_k}$.

Notice that AVG^{λ} is the *mean* operator when $\lambda = 0$ and approaches the *max* operator when $\lambda \to \infty$. These two extreme cases correspond to ranking against the average of all negative pairs and ranking against the single most challenging negative pair, respectively. Empirically, training the models using the *weighted* average ($0 < \lambda \ll \infty$), which assigns larger weights to more challenging negative pairs, stabilizes the training and expedites the convergence.

3.2 Cohesion discriminator: D_{cohesion}

The cohesion discriminator models the cohesion score, which measures how likely two sentences form a cohesive pair of consecutive sentences. Let $s_k := [s_k^1, s_k^2, ..., s_k^n]$ be the kth sentence that consists of n words, $s_{k+1} := [s_{k+1}^1, s_{k+1}^2, ..., s_{k+1}^m]$ be the *real* next sentence that consists of m words, and $\widetilde{s}_{k+1} := [\widetilde{s}_{k+1}^1, \widetilde{s}_{k+1}^2, ..., \widetilde{s}_{k+1}^{\widetilde{m}}]$ be the *artificially constructed incohesive* next sentence that consists of $\widetilde{m}$ words. D_{cohesion} is designed to distinguish a positive (cohesive) pair (s_k, s_{k+1}) from a negative (incohesive) pair $(s_k, \widetilde{s}_{k+1})$ by assigning them with different scores, i.e., $D_{\text{cohesion}}(s_k, s_{k+1}) > D_{\text{cohesion}}(s_k, \widetilde{s}_{k+1})$.

Model architecture. Like the coherence discriminator, this model also takes a form of dual encoder. Given (s_k, s_{k+1}), D_{cohesion} computes the cohesion score in three steps, as illustrated in Figure 1 (lower). The first step is to obtain two sequences of word embedding to represent the two sentences. Then, a pair of source network $u(\cdot)$ and target network $v(\cdot)$ are utilized to encode both s_k and s_{k+1} into two low-dimensional continuous vectors. The two encoders $u(\cdot)$ and $v(\cdot)$ share the same architecture but do *not* share parameters, i.e., $\theta_u \neq \theta_v$, and thus the $D_{\text{cohesion}}\,(s_k, s_{k+1})$ is *not* symmetric. Finally, $D_{\text{cohesion}}\,(s_k, s_{k+1})$ is computed as the cosine similarity of the two vectors.

Note that we use CNNs or RNNs to embed sentences in D_{cohesion}, which takes the word order in a sentence into consideration. This is different from the BOW embedding in the $D_{\text{coherence}}$ where the word order does not matter, because the word order indeed matters when determining the cohesion of two consecutive sentences. As an example from Table 1, for the source sentence *"Once you get there you are greeted by the staff."*, *"They explain everything to you."* is a cohesive follow-up while *"You explain everything to them."* is not.

The parameters of D_{cohesion}, θ_u and θ_v are optimized using the same pairwise ranking loss. The positive pairs (a training minibatch) for D_{cohesion} is obtained from (1) decomposing each paragraph (S, T) in $\{(S_i, T_i)\}_{i=1}^B$ into pairs of consecutive sentences and (2) randomly selecting B pairs as the positive (cohesive) pairs $\{(s_k, s_{k+1})_i\}_{i=1}^B$. We construct negative (incohesive) pairs using the same methods as in the coherence discriminator.

Constructing negative (incohesive) pairs. We construct $2*B-1$ negative pairs $\{(s_k, \widetilde{s}_{k+1,j})_i\}_{j=1}^{2B-1}$ for *every* positive pair $(s_k, s_{k+1})_i$ using three different methods and omit the minibatch index i hereafter. For each positive pair (s_k, s_{k+1}) in the minibatch:

- We mismatch sentence pairs to obtain $\{(s_k, \tilde{s}_{k+1,j})\}_{j=1}^{B-1}$.
- We shuffle words in s_{k+1} to obtain $\tilde{s}_{k+1}$.
- We combine the previous two methods and obtain additional pairs $\{(s_k, \tilde{s}_{k+1,j})\}_{j=1}^{B-1}$.

In total, we obtain $2B - 1$ negative pairs for each positive pair in the minibatch.

Training using a pairwise ranking loss. The parameters of $u(\cdot)$ and $v(\cdot)$ are optimized such that $D_{\text{cohesion}}(s_k, s_{k+1}) > D_{\text{cohesion}}(s_k, \tilde{s}_{k+1,j})$ for any j. To achieve this, we propose to minimize the following pairwise ranking loss with margin δ:

$$L_{\text{cohesion}}(\theta_u, \theta_v) := \max\Big(0, \delta - D_{\text{cohesion}}(s_k, s_{k+1}) + \text{AVG}^{\lambda}\big(\{D_{\text{cohesion}}(s_k, \tilde{s}_{k+1,j})\}_{j=1}^{2B-1}\big)\Big). \tag{2}$$

We leave the training details and hyper-parameter configurations to Section 5.2.

4 Negative-Critical Sequence Training for Long-form Text Generation

4.1 Long-form text generator: G

The generator G is an attention-based bidirectional sequence-to-sequence model (Bahdanau et al., 2014) and is pre-trained by maximizing the log likelihood on training data, which we denote as G_{MLE}. However, long-form texts generated using G_{MLE} often do not meet our high coherence and cohesion standards.

We propose to use the two pre-trained discriminators, $D_{\text{coherence}}$ and D_{cohesion}, to modify the text generation behavior of G_{MLE}. The scores from the discriminators are used as reward (or penalty) signals to adjust the parameters of G_{MLE} using a variant of policy gradient, called *negative-critical sequence training*, which we propose for our task and describe in details in the next subsection.

4.2 Negative-critical sequence training

For an arbitrary pair of S and T_{gen}, where T_{gen} is the generator's output conditioned on S, we compute the coherence and cohesion scores by calling $D_{\text{coherence}}$ and D_{cohesion}. Since each generated text consists of multiple sentences, the overall cohesion score is computed as the mean of all the consecutive sentence pairs, $(s_k, s_{k+1}) \subset [S_{-1}, T_{gen}]$, where S_{-1} is the last sentence from the source.

These scalar scores, however, are not interpretable since the discriminators are trained by optimizing a pairwise ranking loss. Instead, the differences between positive pair scores and the maximal or average negative pair scores provide insights of how well the models distinguish between the positive and the negative pairs.

This difference relates to reward with baseline in actor-critic methods (Barto et al., 1983; Witten, 1977; Williams, 1992; Sutton et al., 1999) that typically require a separate critic function as a baseline. In NLP, we have observed similar practices by Ranzato et al. (2015), Bahdanau et al. (2016), and Nguyen et al. (2017). Rennie et al. (2017) proposed a method that avoids learning a separate critic. Similarly, our method does not require learning a separate critic since this margin is a form of reward minus baseline. Specifically, we define the reward functions with baselines as:

$$R_{\text{coherence}}(S, T_{gen}) := D_{\text{coherence}}(S, T_{gen}) - \mathbb{E}_{\tilde{T}}\left[D_{\text{coherence}}(S, \tilde{T})\right] \tag{3}$$

$$R_{\text{cohesion}}([S_{-1}, T_{gen}]) := \frac{1}{|T_{gen}|} \sum_{\substack{(s_k, s_{k+1}) \\ \subset [S_{-1}, T_{gen}]}} D_{\text{cohesion}}(s_k, s_{k+1}) - \mathbb{E}_{\tilde{s}_{k+1}} \Bigg|_{\substack{(s_k, s_{k+1}) \\ \subset [S, T]}} \left[D_{\text{cohesion}}(s_k, \tilde{s}_{k+1})\right] \tag{4}$$

where $|T_{gen}|$ denotes the number of sentences in T_{gen}, and $\mathbb{E}_{\tilde{T}}$ (and $\mathbb{E}_{\tilde{s}_{k+1}}$) are computed by averaging over an ensemble of negative pairs.

Notice that this reward resembles the ranking loss we use to train our discriminators, except that our baseline is the mean score (instead of the weighted mean) over negative pairs. The rationale for this difference is that: because the best artificially constructed negative sample may be a *formidably* good sample, the maximal or the weighted mean can in fact be noisy as a baseline and thus introduce noise in rewards. To alleviate such noise, we use the *mean discriminator score* of negative pairs as the baseline, and this turns out to be an empirically better alternative. Then we use policy gradient to maximize a weighted sum of the coherence and cohesion rewards.

5 Experiments

In this section, we detail the training and evaluation of $D_{\text{coherence}}$, D_{cohesion}, the baseline generator G_{MLE}, and the RL-tuned generators $G_{\text{MLE+RL(cohesion)}}$, $G_{\text{MLE+RL(coherence)}}$, and

source	**cohesion**	**coherence**
this hotel was unbelievably overpriced .	0.0002	
we were looking for something cheaper but thought we would at least be staying in a decent hotel having paid that much when booking .	0.0411	
it wasn t clear when booking that we would have to share a bathroom .	0.0084	
there was one shower for the whole floor which was tiny and unclean .	0.0054	
the room was old and lacking in facilities .		
target		
the beds were very uncomfortable and the linen was very old .	0.0768	
breakfast was ok , but the staff were incompetent .	0.0591	
on our last day they were too lazy to clean our table and never bothered taking our order .	-0.0097	**+0.3735**
we had to leave having had no breakfast , as we ran out of time .	0.0457	
they saw us get up and leave and didn t even apologise for the appalling lack of service .		
negative target		
the staff recommended great restaurants with very reasonable prices within walking distance .	0.0514	
the paris hop on bus stops nearby .	0.0798	
the gare l est is within 3 blocks .	-0.0156	
we paid 75 euro per nite excluding breakfast but paid for breakfast one day and found it very good and reasonably priced .	0.0082	**-0.2001**
the rooms are clean and bathrooms ensuite .		
more examples of cohesion		
once you get there you are greeted by the staff . they explain everything to you , and in english , not the best , but good enough .	0.1004	
the coffee was even good for a coffee snob like myself . the hotel is much smaller than i thought and only has six floors .	-0.1103	
the only negative was the curtain in the bathroom . it was very shear and we felt that people in the building across the street could look right in at night .	0.0787	
the beer at the lobby bar was stale . there are many friendly cats on the grounds .	-0.0830	

Table 1: Coherence and cohesion rewards on test data. The cohesion reward at the end of each line is computed with its next sentence. This is an example of contradiction and inconsistent sentiment, suggestive of incoherence. We append more examples with extreme cohesion rewards.

TripAdvisor		**Target Sentences Retrieval**		
Discriminators	**Encoding**	**R@1**	**R@5**	**R@10**
$D_{\text{coherence}}$	$\text{Conv}^{512}_{2,3,4,5}$	0.18	0.43	0.60
	$\text{GRU}^{1024}_{\text{1-layer, bi-dir.}}$	**0.26**	**0.50**	**0.65**
D_{cohesion}	$\text{Conv}^{512}_{3,4,5,6}$	**0.12**	**0.28**	**0.43**
	$\text{GRU}^{1024}_{\text{1-layer, bi-dir.}}$	0.11	0.21	0.33

Yelp		**Target Sentences Retrieval**		
Discriminators	**Encoding**	**R@1**	**R@5**	**R@10**
$D_{\text{coherence}}$	$\text{Conv}^{512}_{2,3,4,5}$	0.33	0.61	0.74
	$\text{GRU}^{1024}_{\text{1-layer, bi-dir.}}$	**0.39**	**0.68**	**0.81**
D_{cohesion}	$\text{Conv}^{512}_{3,4,5,6}$	**0.14**	**0.33**	**0.47**
	$\text{GRU}^{1024}_{\text{1-layer, bi-dir.}}$	0.11	0.26	0.39

Table 2: Retrieval ratios for coherence and cohesion discriminators from a collection of 100 negative candidates from the test data. The reported numbers are the averages over 20 evaluations. Notations: $\text{Conv}^{512}_{2,3,4,5}$ is a convolutional input encoder with filter sizes 2, 3, 4, and 5, and there are 512 filters for each filter size. $\text{GRU}^{1024}_{\text{1-layer, bi-dir.}}$ is a 1-layered bi-directional GRU input encoder with hidden size 1024. We experimented different configurations for both encoder types, and selected the best performing models for the negative-critical sequence training step.

$G_{\text{MLE+RL(coherence, cohesion)}}$. We show that, by using feedback from the discriminators, the quality of the generated texts is significantly improved. See Table 3 for a sample comparison.

5.1 Dataset

We use the TripAdvisor hotel English reviews dataset collected by Wang et al. (2010) and the Yelp English reviews dataset[3]. We use only the

[3]https://www.yelp.com/dataset

source sentences	the hotel inglaterra delivered as promised . the staff was welcoming and spoke good english . the cleaning staff did a very good job every day . the rooms were spotless and very modern . the bathroom was large and had a very nice shower , and there were two generously sized bath towels that were twice the size of normal towels .
G_{MLE}	the breakfast in the morning was delicious and very good . it was the only hotel where i slept very well . the staff was very helpful in late afternoon or late times . the breakfast was adequate , with a decent range of cereals , fruit , and fruits . there is also free use of the coffee in the reception area .
$G_{\text{MLE+RL(coherence, cohesion)}}$	the breakfast was plentiful including fresh breads and cooked to order . the location was fantastic . it is in the north of the marina and in a very short distance . the marina has a small swimming pool with sitting area and a small gym . they are very popular and guests have an evening reception which is very nice .

Table 3: Sample generations from our MLE-trained baseline model, G_{MLE}, and our discriminator-guided model $G_{\text{MLE+RL(coherence, cohesion)}}$. The red texts highlight a common problem in G_{MLE} - it exhibits a repetition, and an inconsistent opinion as a review. In contrast, our discriminator-guided model is able to generate a more interesting, and sentiment-consistent continuation.

	Model	NLL	PPL	BLEU-3	BLEU-4	BLEU-5	intra-unique-1	intra-unique-2	inter-unique-2	inter-unique-3	length ratio
TripAdvisor	G_{MLE} (baseline)	0.86	2.36	0.38	0.19	0.08	0.66	0.93	0.40	0.72	1.08
	$G_{\text{MLE +RL(cohesion)}}$	**0.77**	**2.18**	**0.46**	**0.27**	**0.14**	0.64	0.94	0.38	0.71	0.97
	$G_{\text{MLE+RL(coherence)}}$	0.80	2.24	0.44	0.25	0.12	0.64	0.94	0.39	0.72	1.06
	$G_{\text{MLE+RL(coherence, cohesion)}}$	0.80	2.25	0.44	0.24	0.12	0.65	0.94	0.40	0.72	1.02

	Model	NLL	PPL	BLEU-3	BLEU-4	BLEU-5	intra-unique-1	intra-unique-2	inter-unique-2	inter-unique-3	length ratio
Yelp	G_{MLE} (baseline)	1.32	3.84	0.37	0.17	0.07	0.68	0.95	0.54	0.86	1.07
	$G_{\text{MLE+RL(cohesion)}}$	1.26	3.65	**0.45**	**0.23**	**0.11**	0.68	0.95	0.53	0.85	1.05
	$G_{\text{MLE+RL(coherence)}}$	**1.24**	**3.56**	0.45	0.23	0.11	0.69	0.95	0.55	0.87	1.00
	$G_{\text{MLE+RL(coherence, cohesion)}}$	1.25	3.59	0.43	0.22	0.11	0.69	0.95	0.56	0.88	1.05

Table 4: An ablation study with automated evaluation metric scores: NLL, PPL, BLEU-n, intra/inter-unique-n, along with the length ratio with the length of corresponding true target sentences as 1. Significant numbers are highlighted in **bold** before rounding.

subsets of the two datasets that satisfy the following two conditions: (1) a review must have at least 10 sentences, and (2) each sentence has from 5 to 30 words. This yields roughly 60,000 TripAdvisor reviews and 220,000 Yelp reviews, split into $[0.8, 0.1, 0.1]$ ratio for train/dev/test sets.

We merge the source and target vocabularies, and limit it to the top 50,000 frequent words, excluding special tokens. For each review, we use the first five sentences as the input S to G, and the next five sentences as the target output T from G.

5.2 Implementation details

Baseline G_{MLE}. G_{MLE} takes individual words as inputs and embeds into a pre-trained GloVe 300-dimensional word vectors. This embedding layer is fixed throughout training. G_{MLE} uses a two-layered GRU and hidden size of 1024 for both encoder and decoder. During optimization using Adam (Kingma and Ba, 2014), we set the learning rate to 2e-4 and clip the gradient's L2-norm to 1.0. We initially train G_{MLE} for 60 epochs on the TripAdvisor data and 30 epochs on the Yelp data.

Discriminators. For the CNN-based encoder, the convolutional layer consists of filters of sizes 2, 3, 4, and 5 for $D_{\text{coherence}}$ (3, 4, 5, and 6 for D_{cohesion}), each with 512 filters. Each convolution filter is followed by a $\tanh$ activation. Then, we max-pool in time and append a fully connected layer to generate a feature vector of dimension 512, followed by a batch normalization layer and a $\tanh$ activation. For the RNN-based encoder, we use a 1-layered bi-directional GRU, concatenate the final hidden states at both ends, and append the same remaining layers.

Both discriminators use the pre-trained GloVe word embedding vectors[4], which are fixed during the training. We use an Adam optimizer with a learning rate of 1e-5. We fix $\lambda = 2$ and $\delta = 0.2$ in equations (1) and (2).[5] We train both discriminators for 50 epochs and choose the models with the best R@1 scores on the validation dataset.

Model $G_{\text{MLE+RL}}$. In the fine-tuning stage, we use the negative-critical sequence training method,

[4]The vector dimension can be different from that of G. The differences were marginal for sizes 50, 100, and 300. For results shown in this paper, we used the same dimension of size 300.

[5]We performed a coarse grid search over the values of λ and δ and these values for the hyper-parameters pair resulted in fast convergence to high recall scores on the dev dataset.

Cohesion						Coherence					
Human judges preferred:						*Human judges preferred:*					
Our Method		Neutral	Comparison			Our Method		Neutral	Comparison		
$G_{\text{MLE+RL}}$	**36.41%**	33.57%	30.50%	G_{MLE}		$G_{\text{MLE+RL}}$	**37.23%**	31.44%	31.80%	G_{MLE}	
$G_{\text{MLE+RL}}$	29.91%	30.85%	**39.24%**	Human		$G_{\text{MLE+RL}}$	28.96%	31.32%	**39.72%**	Human	

Table 5: Results of **Human Evaluation** showing preferences (%) for our model $G_{\text{MLE+RL(coherence, cohesion)}}$ vis-a-vis the baseline G_{MLE} after adjustment for spamming. $G_{\text{MLE+RL(coherence, cohesion)}}$ is preferred over G_{MLE}. For simplicity, the 5-point Likert scale has been collapsed to a 3-point scale. See the Appendix for further details of distributions.

as described in Section 4, up to 5 epochs, with a learning rate of 1e-5. We equally weight the coherence and cohesion rewards, $\frac{1}{2}R_{\text{coherence}}(S, T_{gen}) + \frac{1}{2}R_{\text{cohesion}}([S_{-1}, T_{gen}])$. We also continue the supervised learning of G to constrain the policy search within a space that represents the sentences that are likely to be grammatically plausible, similar to Paulus et al. (2017); Wu et al. (2016); Lewis et al. (2017). For all the generations from G_{MLE} and $G_{\text{MLE+RL}}$, we use the simple greedy decoding method because we do not observe any significant difference when switching to beam search.

5.3 Results

Evaluating $D_{\text{coherence}}$ and D_{cohesion}. Since the discriminators are implemented as pairwise rankers, we employ the metrics commonly used in information retrieval for evaluation, i.e., recall at *K* (R@*K*), which is defined as the fraction of correctly identifying an item in the TOP-*K* retrieved list (Baeza-Yates and Ribeiro-Neto, 1999). We present the retrieval results in Table 2. To help readers understand the roles of $D_{\text{coherence}}$ and D_{cohesion}, we present examples of positive and negative pairs and their rewards in Table 1.

Automatic evaluation of G. It is widely known that there is no perfect automated metric to evaluate text generators. Nevertheless, we report the scores of widely used metrics, including negative log-likelihood (NLL), perplexity (PPL), BLEU and the proportion of unique n-grams within a single generation (intra-unique-n), and across generations (inter-unique-n), as in Gu et al. (2018). Results in Table 4 show that our discriminators significantly improve BLEU scores, NLL and PPL, with marginal difference in diversity.

Human evaluation of G. Coherence and cohesion of a text cannot be easily measured using standard automated metrics. Thus, we perform crowd-sourced human evaluation. We randomly selected 200 samples from the TripAdvisor dataset, including corresponding generated output from the baseline G_{MLE} and our model $G_{\text{MLE+RL}}$. For comparison, we pair systems as (*Human* $\leftrightarrow G_{\text{MLE+RL}}$) and ($G_{\text{MLE+RL}} \leftrightarrow G_{\text{MLE}}$).

The outputs of these system pairs are presented in random order and each is ranked in terms of coherence and cohesion using a five-point Likert scale by human judges. Initially, we hired 7 judges to judge each pair. We identified a group of poor judges (probable spammers) who choose $G_{\text{MLE+RL}}$ over the *Human* more than 40% of the time, and eliminated them from the judge pool. Table 5 reports the final scores in terms of percentages of the total remaining judgments.

6 Conclusion

This paper proposes a neural approach to explicitly modeling cross-sentence linguistic properties, coherence and cohesion, for long-form text generation. The coherence discriminator $D_{\text{coherence}}$ provides a macro-level view on structuring a paragraph. The cohesion discriminator D_{cohesion} provides a micro-level view on local connectivity between neighboring sentences. The pre-trained discriminators are used to score the generated texts and artificially constructed negative pair scores are used to form baselines for the policy gradient, which we call negative-critical sequence training, to train neural language models.

On two long-form text generation tasks, human evaluation results are consistent with automatic evaluation results, which together demonstrate that our proposed method generates more locally and globally consistent texts with the help of the discriminators.

Despite the encouraging initial results, we only scratched the surface of the problem. The proposed method is yet to be significantly improved to meet the ultimate goal of generating meaningful and logical long-form texts.

References

Sanjeev Arora, Yingyu Liang, and Tengyu Ma. 2017. A simple but tough-to-beat baseline for sentence embeddings. In *International Conference on Learning Representations*.

Ricardo Baeza-Yates and Berthier Ribeiro-Neto. 1999. *Modern information retrieval*, volume 463. ACM Press Books.

Dzmitry Bahdanau, Philemon Brakel, Kelvin Xu, Anirudh Goyal, Ryan Lowe, Joelle Pineau, Aaron Courville, and Yoshua Bengio. 2016. An actor-critic algorithm for sequence prediction. *arXiv preprint arXiv:1607.07086*.

Dzmitry Bahdanau, Kyunghyun Cho, and Yoshua Bengio. 2014. Neural machine translation by jointly learning to align and translate. *CoRR*, abs/1409.0473.

Andrew G Barto, Richard S Sutton, and Charles W Anderson. 1983. Neuronlike adaptive elements that can solve difficult learning control problems. *IEEE transactions on systems, man, and cybernetics*, SMC-13(5):834–846.

Regina Barzilay and Mirella Lapata. 2008. Modeling local coherence: An entity-based approach. *Computational Linguistics*, 34(1):1–34.

Antoine Bosselut, Asli Celikyilmaz, Xiaodong He, Jianfeng Gao, Po-Sen Huang, and Yejin Choi. 2018. Discourse-aware neural rewards for coherent text generation. In *Proc. of NAACL*, pages 173–184.

Kyunghyun Cho, Bart van Merriënboer, Çalar Gülçehre, Dzmitry Bahdanau, Fethi Bougares, Holger Schwenk, and Yoshua Bengio. 2014. Learning phrase representations using rnn encoder–decoder for statistical machine translation. In *EMNLP*.

Philip R Cohen and Hector J Levesque. 1985. Speech acts and rationality. In *Proceedings of the 23rd annual meeting on Association for Computational Linguistics*, pages 49–60. Association for Computational Linguistics.

Ronan Collobert, Jason Weston, Léon Bottou, Michael Karlen, Koray Kavukcuoglu, and Pavel Kuksa. 2011. Natural language processing (almost) from scratch. *J. Mach. Learn. Res.*, 12:2493–2537.

Dan Cristea, Nancy Ide, and Laurent Romary. 1998. Veins theory: A model of global discourse cohesion and coherence. In *Proceedings of the 36th Annual Meeting of the Association for Computational Linguistics and 17th International Conference on Computational Linguistics-Volume 1*, pages 281–285. Association for Computational Linguistics.

Hal Daumé, John Langford, and Daniel Marcu. 2009. Search-based structured prediction. *CoRR*, abs/0907.0786.

Harold P Edmundson. 1969. New methods in automatic extracting. *Journal of the ACM (JACM)*, 16(2):264–285.

William Fedus, Ian Goodfellow, and Andrew Dai. 2018. MaskGAN: Better text generation via filling in the ____. In *ICLR*.

Jianfeng Gao, Michel Galley, and Lihong Li. 2018. Neural approaches to conversational AI. *arXiv preprint arXiv:1809.08267*.

Jianfeng Gao, Patrick Pantel, Michael Gamon, Xiaodong He, and Li Deng. 2014. Modeling interestingness with deep neural networks. In *Proceedings of the 2014 Conference on Empirical Methods in Natural Language Processing (EMNLP)*, pages 2–13.

Yunchao Gong, Yangqing Jia, Thomas Leung, Alexander Toshev, and Sergey Ioffe. 2013. Deep convolutional ranking for multilabel image annotation. *arXiv preprint arXiv:1312.4894*.

Ian Goodfellow, Jean Pouget-Abadie, Mehdi Mirza, Bing Xu, David Warde-Farley, Sherjil Ozair, Aaron Courville, and Yoshua Bengio. 2014. Generative adversarial nets. In *Advances in Neural Information Processing Systems 27*, pages 2672–2680.

Alex Graves. 2013. Generating sequences with recurrent neural networks. *arXiv preprint arXiv:1308.0850*.

Xiaodong Gu, Kyunghyun Cho, JungWoo Ha, and Sunghun Kim. 2018. DialogWAE: Multimodal response generation with conditional wasserstein auto-encoder. *CoRR*, abs/1805.12352.

Jiaxian Guo, Sidi Lu, Han Cai, Weinan Zhang, Yong Yu, and Jun Wang. 2017. Long text generation via adversarial training with leaked information. *arXiv preprint arXiv:1709.08624*.

M Halliday and Ruqaiya Hasan. 1996. Cohesion in text.

Jerry R Hobbs. 1985. On the coherence and structure of discourse.

Ari Holtzman, Jan Buys, Maxwell Forbes, Antoine Bosselut, David Golub, and Yejin Choi. 2018. Learning to write with cooperative discriminators. In *Proceedings of the Association for Computational Linguistics*.

Eduard H Hovy. 1988. Planning coherent multisentential text. In *Proceedings of the 26th annual meeting on Association for Computational Linguistics*, pages 163–169. Association for Computational Linguistics.

Eduard H Hovy. 1991. Approaches to the planning of coherent text. In *Natural language generation in artificial intelligence and computational linguistics*, pages 83–102. Springer.

Po-Sen Huang, Xiaodong He, Jianfeng Gao, Li Deng, Alex Acero, and Larry P. Heck. 2013. Learning deep structured semantic models for web search using clickthrough data. In *CIKM*.

Yoon Kim. 2014. Convolutional neural networks for sentence classification. In *EMNLP*.

Diederik P. Kingma and Jimmy Ba. 2014. Adam: A method for stochastic optimization. *CoRR*, abs/1412.6980.

Mike Lewis, Denis Yarats, Yann N Dauphin, Devi Parikh, and Dhruv Batra. 2017. Deal or no deal? end-to-end learning for negotiation dialogues. *arXiv preprint arXiv:1706.05125*.

Jiwei Li, Michel Galley, Chris Brockett, Jianfeng Gao, and Bill Dolan. 2015. A diversity-promoting objective function for neural conversation models. *arXiv preprint arXiv:1510.03055*.

Jiwei Li, Michel Galley, Chris Brockett, Georgios P Spithourakis, Jianfeng Gao, and Bill Dolan. 2016a. A persona-based neural conversation model. *arXiv preprint arXiv:1603.06155*.

Jiwei Li, Will Monroe, Alan Ritter, Michel Galley, Jianfeng Gao, and Dan Jurafsky. 2016b. Deep reinforcement learning for dialogue generation. *arXiv preprint arXiv:1606.01541*.

Jiwei Li, Will Monroe, Tianlin Shi, Sébastien Jean, Alan Ritter, and Dan Jurafsky. 2017. Adversarial learning for neural dialogue generation. *arXiv preprint arXiv:1701.06547*.

Elizabeth DuRoss Liddy. 1991. The discourse-level structure of empirical abstracts: An exploratory study. *Information Processing & Management*, 27(1):55–81.

Chin-Yew Lin and Eduard Hovy. 2003. Automatic evaluation of summaries using n-gram co-occurrence statistics. In *Proceedings of the 2003 Conference of the North American Chapter of the Association for Computational Linguistics on Human Language Technology - Volume 1*, NAACL '03, pages 71–78, Stroudsburg, PA, USA.

Kevin Lin, Dianqi Li, Xiaodong He, Zhengyou Zhang, and Ming-Ting Sun. 2017. Adversarial ranking for language generation. In *Advances in Neural Information Processing Systems*, pages 3155–3165.

Inderjeet Mani, Eric Bloedorn, and Barbara Gates. 1998. Using cohesion and coherence models for text summarization. In *Intelligent Text Summarization Symposium*, pages 69–76.

William C Mann and Sandra A Thompson. 1988. Rhetorical structure theory: Toward a functional theory of text organization. *Text-Interdisciplinary Journal for the Study of Discourse*, 8(3):243–281.

Kathleen R McKeown. 1985. Discourse strategies for generating natural-language text. *Artificial Intelligence*, 27(1):1–41.

Khanh Nguyen, Hal Daumé, and Jordan L. Boyd-Graber. 2017. Reinforcement learning for bandit neural machine translation with simulated human feedback. In *EMNLP*.

H. Palangi, L. Deng, Y. Shen, J. Gao, X. He, J. Chen, X. Song, and R. Ward. 2016. Deep sentence embedding using long short-term memory networks: Analysis and application to information retrieval. *IEEE/ACM Transactions on Audio, Speech, and Language Processing*, 24(4):694–707.

Kishore Papineni, Salim Roukos, Todd Ward, and Wei-Jing Zhu. 2002. BLEU: A method for automatic evaluation of machine translation. In *Proceedings of the 40th Annual Meeting on Association for Computational Linguistics*, ACL '02, pages 311–318.

Romain Paulus, Caiming Xiong, and Richard Socher. 2017. A deep reinforced model for abstractive summarization. *CoRR*, abs/1705.04304.

Jeffrey Pennington, Richard Socher, and Christopher D. Manning. 2014. GloVe: Global vectors for word representation. In *Empirical Methods in Natural Language Processing (EMNLP)*, pages 1532–1543.

Marc'Aurelio Ranzato, Sumit Chopra, Michael Auli, and Wojciech Zaremba. 2015. Sequence level training with recurrent neural networks. *CoRR*, abs/1511.06732.

Steven J. Rennie, Etienne Marcheret, Youssef Mroueh, Jarret Ross, and Vaibhava Goel. 2017. Self-critical sequence training for image captioning. *2017 IEEE Conference on Computer Vision and Pattern Recognition (CVPR)*, pages 1179–1195.

Lifeng Shang, Zhengdong Lu, and Hang Li. 2015. Neural responding machine for short-text conversation. *arXiv preprint arXiv:1503.02364*.

Alessandro Sordoni, Michel Galley, Michael Auli, Chris Brockett, Yangfeng Ji, Margaret Mitchell, Jian-Yun Nie, Jianfeng Gao, and Bill Dolan. 2015. A neural network approach to context-sensitive generation of conversational responses. In *NAACL-HLT*.

Ilya Sutskever, Oriol Vinyals, and Quoc V Le. 2014. Sequence to sequence learning with neural networks. In *NIPS*, pages 3104–3112.

Richard S. Sutton, David McAllester, Satinder Singh, and Yishay Mansour. 1999. Policy gradient methods for reinforcement learning with function approximation. In *Proceedings of the 12th International Conference on Neural Information Processing Systems*, NIPS'99, pages 1057–1063. MIT Press.

Teun A Van Dijk. 2013. *News as discourse*. Routledge.

Oriol Vinyals and Quoc Le. 2015. A neural conversational model. *ICML Deep Learning Workshop*.

Hongning Wang, Yue Lu, and ChengXiang Zhai. 2010. Latent aspect rating analysis on review text data: a rating regression approach. In *KDD*.

John Wieting, Mohit Bansal, Kevin Gimpel, and Karen Livescu. 2016. Towards universal paraphrastic sentence embeddings. *ICLR*.

J.M. Williams and G.G. Colomb. 1995. *Style: Toward Clarity and Grace*. Chicago guides to writing, editing, and publishing. University of Chicago Press.

Ronald J. Williams. 1992. Simple statistical gradient-following algorithms for connectionist reinforcement learning. *Mach. Learn.*, 8(3-4):229–256.

Ian H Witten. 1977. An adaptive optimal controller for discrete-time markov environments. *Information and control*, 34(4):286–295.

Yonghui Wu, Mike Schuster, Zhifeng Chen, Quoc V Le, Mohammad Norouzi, Wolfgang Macherey, Maxim Krikun, Yuan Cao, Qin Gao, Klaus Macherey, et al. 2016. Google's neural machine translation system: Bridging the gap between human and machine translation. *arXiv preprint arXiv:1609.08144*.

Tao Xu, Pengchuan Zhang, Qiuyuan Huang, Han Zhang, Zhe Gan, Xiaolei Huang, and Xiaodong He. 2017. Attngan: Fine-grained text to image generation with attentional generative adversarial networks. *arXiv preprint*.

Zichao Yang, Zhiting Hu, Chris Dyer, Eric P Xing, and Taylor Berg-Kirkpatrick. 2018. Unsupervised text style transfer using language models as discriminators. *arXiv preprint arXiv:1805.11749*.

Lantao Yu, Weinan Zhang, Jun Wang, and Yong Yu. 2017. SeqGAN: Sequence generative adversarial nets with policy gradient. In *AAAI*.

Yizhe Zhang, Michel Galley, Jianfeng Gao, Zhe Gan, Xiujun Li, Chris Brockett, and Bill Dolan. 2018. Generating informative and diverse conversational responses via adversarial information maximization. In *NIPS*.

Yizhe Zhang, Zhe Gan, Kai Fan, Zhi Chen, Ricardo Henao, Dinghan Shen, and Lawrence Carin. 2017. Adversarial feature matching for text generation. In *NIPS*.

Character Identification Refined: A Proposal

Labiba Jahan & Mark A. Finlayson
School of Computing and Information Sciences
Florida International University
11200 S.W. 8th Street, CASE 362, Miami, FL 33199
{ljaha002, markaf}@fiu.edu

Abstract

Characters are a key element of narrative and so character identification plays an important role in automatic narrative understanding. Unfortunately, most prior work that incorporates character identification is not built upon a clear, theoretically grounded concept of character. They either take character identification for granted (e.g., using simple heuristics on referring expressions), or rely on simplified definitions that do not capture important distinctions between characters and other referents in the story. Prior approaches have also been rather complicated, relying, for example, on predefined case bases or ontologies. In this paper we propose a narratologically grounded definition of character for discussion at the workshop, and also demonstrate a preliminary yet straightforward supervised machine learning model with a small set of features that performs well on two corpora. The most important of the two corpora is a set of 46 Russian folktales, on which the model achieves an F_1 of 0.81. Error analysis suggests that features relevant to the plot will be necessary for further improvements in performance.

Characters are critical to most of definition of narrative. As an example, Monika Fludernik defines a narrative as "a representation of a possible world ... at whose centre there are *one or several protagonists* of an anthropomorphic nature ... who (mostly) perform goal-directed actions ... " (Fludernik, 2009, p.6; emphasis ours). Therefore, if we wish to advance the field of automatic narrative understanding, we must be able to identify the characters in a story.

Numerous prior approaches have incorporated character identification in one way or another. Some approaches, e.g., examining charaters' social networks (e.g., Sack, 2013), take character identification for granted, implementing heuristic-driven identification approaches over named entities or coreference chains that are not examined for their efficacy. Other approaches have sought to solve the character identification task specifically, but have relied on domain-specific ontologies (e.g., Declerck et al., 2012) or complicated case bases (e.g., Valls-Vargas et al., 2014). Others have taken supervised machine learning approaches (Calix et al., 2013). Regardless, all of the prior work has, unfortunately, had a relatively impoverished view of what a character is, from a narratological point of view. In particular, a key aspect of any character is that it *contributes to the plot*; characters are not just any animate entity in the narrative. We outline this idea first, before describing how we constructed two annotated datasets reflecting this narratologically grounded view oharacter. Then we demonstrate a straightforward supervised machine learning model that performs reasonably well on this data. This paper is just a first proposal on this approach, as much remains be done.

The paper proceeds as follows. First we discuss a definition of character drawn from narratology, contrasting this concept with those used in prior computational work (§1). We then describe our data sources and annotation procedures (§2). Next we discuss the experimental setup including the features and classification model (§3). We present the results and analyze the error patterns of the system, discussing various aspects, which leads us to a discussion of future work (§4). Although we have discussed prior work briefly in the introduction, we summarize work related to this study (§5) before we conclude by enumerating our contributions (§6).

1 What is a Character?

All prior works that we have found which incorporate character identification in narrative did not

Proceedings of the First Workshop on Narrative Understanding, pages 12–18
Minneapolis, Minnesota, June 7, 2019.

provide a clear definition of *character*. So far the work that reports the best performance is by Valls-Vargas et al. (2014), where they mentioned different types of characters such as humans, animals (e.g., a talking mouse), anthropomorphic objects (e.g., a magical oven, a talking river), fantastical creatures (e.g., goblins), and characters specific to the folklore (e.g., the Russian characters Morozko and Baba Yaga). Despite this relatively comprehensive list of character examples, they did not provide any properties that distinguish characters from other animate entities.

Consider the follow example. Let's assume we have a story about Mary, a little girl who has a dog named Fido. Mary plays with Fido when she feels lonely. Also, Fido helps Mary in her daily chores and brings letters for Mary from the post office. One day Mary and Fido are walking through town observing the local color. They see a crowd gathered around a fruit vendor; an ugly man crosses the path in front of them; another dog barks at Fido. Many narratologists and lay people would agree that the story has at least two characters, Mary and Fido. Depending on how the story is told, either Mary or Fido may be the protagonist. But what about the other entities mentioned in the story? What about the unnamed man who crosses their path? Is he a character? What about the formless crowd? Is the crowd itself a character, or perhaps its constituent people? What about the fruit vendor, who is hawking his wares? And what about the barking dog? Where do we draw the line?

To clarify these cases, our first goal was to find an appropriate definition of character grounded in narrative theory. We studied different books and literature reviews on narratology that provided different definitions of character. Helpfully, Seymour Chatman, in his classic book "Story and Discourse: Narrative Structure in Fiction and Film" (1986), collected a number of view on character across multiple narratological traditions. Several of the definitions were complex and would be quite difficult to model computationally. Others were too vague to inform computational approaches. However, one definition provided a reasonable target:

> The view of the Formalists and (some) structuralists resemble Aristotle's in a striking way. They too ague that characters are products of plots, that their status is "functional," that they are, in short, participants or *actants* rather than *personnages*, that it is erroneous to consider them as real beings. Narrative theory, they say, must avoid psychological essences; aspects of character can only be "functions." They wish to analyze only what characters do in a story, not what they are—that is, "are" by some outside psychological or moral measure. Further, they maintain that the "spheres of action" in which a character moves are "comparatively small in number, typical and classable." (Chatman, 1986, p.111)

Here, an *actant* is something that plays any of a set of active roles in a narrative and *plot* denotes the main events of a story. This definition, then, though presented via somewhat obscure narratological terminology, gives a fairly conceptually concise definition of a character: A character is *an animate being that is important to the plot.* By this measure then, we are justified in identifying Mary and Fido as characters, but not the various entities they casually encounter in their stroll through town.

2 Data

Armed with this refined definition of character, we proceeded to generate preliminary data that could be used to explore this idea and demonstrate the feasibility of training a supervised machine learning system for this concept of character. We sought to explore how easily computable features, like those used in prior work, could capture this slightly refined concept of character. We began with the fact that characters and other entities are expressed in texts as coreference chains made up of referring expressions (Jurafsky and Martin, 2007). Thus any labeling of *character* must apply to coreference chains. We generated character annotations on two corpora, one with 46 texts (the extended ProppLearning corpus) and other with 94 texts (a subset of the InScript corpus), for a total of 1,147 characters and 127,680 words.

The ProppLearner corpus was constructed for other work on learning plot functions (Finlayson, 2017). The corpus that was reported in that paper comprised only 15 Russian folktales, but we obtained the extended set of 46 tales from the authors. These tales were originally collected in

	Texts	Tokens	Coreference Chains Total	Anim.	Inanim.	Char.	Non-Char.
ProppLearner (Ext.)	46	109,120	4,950	2,004	2,946	1,047	1,361
Inscript (Subset)	94	18,568	615	105	510	94	521
Total	140	127,680	5,565	2,098	3,467	1,141	1,882

Table 1: Counts across coreference chains of different categories, as well as texts and tokens.

Coreference Chain Head	Class	Explanation
Nikita, tsar	Character	People who perform as a character
he, she, her	Character	Animate pronouns that perform as a character
walking stove, talking tree	Character	Inanimate entities that perform as a character
a bird, insects	Non Character	Animate entities that does not perform as a character

Table 2: Examples of annotation of characters in coreference chain level.

Russian in the late 1800's but translated into English within the past 70 years. All of the texts in the corpus already had gold-standard annotations for major characters, congruent with our proposed definition. Usefully, the corpus also has gold-standard annotations for referring expressions, coreference chains, and animacy.

We also investigated the InScript corpus (Modi et al., 2017). InScript contains 1,000 stories comprising approximately 200,000 words, where each story describes some stereotypical human activity such as going to a restaurant or visiting a doctor. We selected a subset (94 stories, approximately 19k tokens) of the corpus that describes activity of taking a bath. It has referring expressions and coreference chains already annotated.

The first author manually annotated both of these corpora as to whether each coreference chain acted as a character in the story. According to the definition mentioned above, we marked a chain as character if it is animate and participates in the plot of the story. Because this is a preliminary study, we have not yet done double annotation; this will done as be future work. According to our definition, characters must be animate; thus, because the ProppLearner corpus provides gold-standard animacy markings, on that corpus we only assessed whether animate chains represented characters. The InScript corpus did not come with animacy markings, and so we assessed every coreference chain. The stories in the InScript corpus are fairly simple, and usually only involve a single protagonist, alone in the story. Because of this, every single animate chain in that data was also a character, and both automatic animacy detection and character detection worked extremely well; as we will discuss later, this is rather uniformative. Table 1 shows the total number of texts and tokens in each corpus, as well as a breakdown of various categories of coreference chain: animate, inanimate, character, and non-character. Table 2 gives some examples of character annotations.

3 Approach

Because to be a character a referent must actively involved in the plot, characters are necessarily animate, although clearly not all animate things are necessarily characters. Animacy is the characteristic of independently carrying out actions in the story world (e.g., movement or communication) (Jahan et al., 2018). Therefore detecting the animacy of coreference chains will immediately narrow the set of possibilities for character detection. Our character identification system thus consists of two stages: first, we detect animate chains from the coreference chains using an existing animacy detector (§3.1); second, we apply a supervised machine learning model that identifies which of those chains qualify as characters (§3.2).

3.1 Animate Chain Detection

Our first step was to identify animate chains. In order to do that we used a coreference animacy detector described in prior work (Jahan et al., 2018). This model is a hybrid system incorporating both supervised machine learning and hand-built rules, and achieves state-of-the-art performance. The extended ProppLearner corpus came with animacy

Corpus	Acc.	Inanimate κ	Inanimate Prec.	Inanimate Rec.	Inanimate F_1	Animate κ	Animate Prec.	Animate Rec.	Animate F_1
ProppLearner	85%	0.72	0.93	0.82	0.87	0.72	0.78	0.92	0.84
InScript	99%	0.99	0.99	0.99	0.99	0.99	0.99	0.99	0.99

Table 3: Performance of the animacy model on the corpora.

Corpus	Feature Set	Acc.	Non Character κ	Non Character Prec.	Non Character Rec.	Non Character F_1	Character κ	Character Prec.	Character Rec.	Character F_1
Propp-Learner	Baseline MFC	56%	0.0	0.57	1.0	0.72	0.0	0.0	0.0	0.0
	SS, WN, NE	80%	0.82	1.0	0.87	0.93	0.64	0.75	0.80	0.77
	WN, CL	80%	0.82	1.0	0.87	0.92	0.64	0.75	0.80	0.78
	CL, SS, WN	84%	0.78	1.0	0.84	0.92	0.66	0.75	0.84	0.79
	CL, WN, NE	82%	0.81	0.86	0.92	0.92	0.64	0.82	0.77	0.80
	CL, SS, WN	84%	0.78	1.0	0.84	0.92	0.66	0.75	0.84	0.79
	CL, SS, WN, NE	85%	0.78	1.0	0.85	0.91	0.66	0.88	0.76	**0.81**
InScript	CL, SS, WN, NE	99%	0.99	0.99	0.99	0.99	0.99	0.99	0.99	**0.99**

Table 4: Performance of different features sets for identifying characters. MFC = most frequent class. κ = Cohen's kappa (Cohen, 1960)

already marked; the InScript corpus already has gold standard coreference chains, and so we used those coreference annotations as input to the animacy model to generate animacy markings. The performance of the animacy model on both corpora is shown in Table 3.

3.2 Feature Selection for Character Identification

We used four different features for our character identification model.

1. **Coreference Chain Length (CL)**: We computed the length of a coreference chain as an integer feature. This feature explicitly captures the tendency of the long chains to be characters, as discussed in prior work (Eisenberg and Finlayson, 2017).

2. **Semantic Subject (SS)**: We also computed whether or not the head of a coreference chain appeared as a semantic subject (ARG0) to a verb, and encoded this as a boolean feature. We used the semantic role labeler associated with the Story Workbench annotation tool (Finlayson, 2008, 2011) to compute semantic roles for all the verbs in the stories.

3. **Named Entity (NE)**: We computed whether or not the head of a coreference chain appeared was a named entity with the category *PERSON*, and encoded this as a boolean feature. The named entities were computed using the classic API of the Stanford dependency parse (Manning et al., 2014, v3.7.0).

4. **WordNet (WN)**: We checked if the head of a coreference chain is a descendant of *person* in WordNet, and encoded this as a boolean feature.

3.3 Classification Model

Our classification model is straightforward supervised machine learning, in which we explored different combinations of our features. We implemented our model using an SVM (Chang and Lin, 2011) with a Radial Basis Function Kernel[1]. We tested different combinations of features on the ProppLearner corpus, and their relative performances are shown in Table 4. The best performing feature set was using all four features, and we also tested this model on the InScript data. We trained each model using ten-fold cross validation, and report macroaverages across the performance on the test folds.

4 Results, Error Analysis, & Discussion

The best model, using all four features, achieves an F_1 of 0.81 on the ProppLearner data, and an F_1 of 0.99 on the InScript data. The result on the InScript data is misleadingly high and deserves some

[1] SVM parameters were set at $\gamma = 1$, $C = 0.5$ and $p = 1$.

discussion. The InScript stories are quite simple, only told in the first person, and usually featuring only a single animate referent who is also the protagonist. Therefore the almost exclusive reference to characters in these stories was the personal pronoun *I*. Thus both the animacy detector and the character identifier had much higher performance than one would expect on more complicated stories.

A detailed error analysis of the results on the ProppLearner data revealed at least three major problems for the character identification model.

First, the character model relied on the output of the animacy model, and so if a character was not marked animate, the character model also missed it. Conversely, sometimes inanimate chains are incorrectly marked animate, providing an additional opportunity for the character model to err. Thus, in order to improve the performance of our character model, we have to improve the performance of the animacy model.

Second, it is hard to detect a character chain with a very few mentions. To solve this problem we could possibly add some new features related to events of the story because event patterns can be helpful to find a character.

Third, some non-character animate entities were incorrectly identified as characters, because there is strong correlation between animacy and character. To solve this problem we need more analysis of the plot structure and to find features that more specific to character vis-a-vis animacy.

The last point is critical. Although it seems that features related to how animate and prevalent a referent is are quite useful for identifying characters, they still fall somewhat short. We hypothesize that features related to encoding aspects of the plot, to determine if a referent is contributing to the plot in a meaningful way, will be critical to substantially improving character identification performance. We plan to explore this idea in future work.

5 Related Work

The most relevant prior work is a case based reasoning (CBR) system called *Voz* (Valls-Vargas et al., 2014). Voz could identify characters in unannotated narrative text and achieved an accuracy of 93.5%. The system relied on 193 different features. They also proposed a new similarity measure called *Continuous Jaccard* to measure the similarity between a given entity and those in the case base. Although quite useful, this system does not give a theoretically grounded definition of character, and the CBR system is quite complicated.

Calix et al. (2013) developed a model to detect sentient actors in spoken stories. This is akin to animacy detection. They implemented a SVM classifier using 4 categories of features: syntactic, knowledge-based, relation to pronouns, and general context based. Their model achieved 0.86 F_1 score, but, because they are focusing on animacy, they are only detecting a set of entities that contain the characters, not the characters themselves.

Declerck et al. (2012) used an ontology-based method to detect characters in folktales. Their ontology consists of family relations as well as elements of folktales such as supernatural entities. After looking at the heads of noun phrases and comparing them with labels in the ontology, they added the noun phrase to the ontology as a potential character if a match was found. Then, they applied inference rules to the candidate characters in order to find two strings in the text that refer to the same character. They discarded strings that were related only once to a potential character and were not involved in an action. They obtained an accuracy of 79%, a precision of 0.88, a recall 0.73, and an F_1 of 0.80. Their implicit definition character is most similar to ours, but their ontology based approach is domain specific. As with most domain specific approaches, it would likely not generalize easily to other domains.

Goh et al. (2012) implemented a rule-based system using verbs and WordNet in order to determine the protagonists in fairy tales (where protagonists must by necessity be animate). This is a related task, but not exactly the same as full character identification. They used the Stanford parser's phrase structure trees to obtain the subjects and objects of the verbs and used the dependency structure to obtain the head noun of compound phrases. Additionally, they used WordNet's *derivationally related* relation to find verbs associated with a particular nominal action. They achieved a precision of 0.69, a recall of 0.75, and an F_1 of 0.67.

Mamede and Chaleira (2004) developed a system to identify which entities were responsible for the direct and indirect discourses found in children stories. Again, this is a related task but not the same as character identification. They achieved an accuracy of 84.8% on the training corpus, and 65.7% on the test corpus. Similarly, Zhang et al. (2003) developed a system to identify speakers of the children's story for speech synthesis. In this system they automatically identified quoted texts and assigned speaker to each quote. They did not report the exact performance of their system.

Bamman et al. (2014) developed a hierarchical Bayesian approach to infer latent character types automatically in a collection of 15,099 English novels published between 1700 and 1899. First, they implemented character clustering and then generated related texts to a character to decide which persona a particular character embodies.

Vala et al. (2015) implemented an eight stage pipeline incorporating NER, coreference chains, a series of name variation rules, and WordNet senses to identify characters in literary texts, achieving an an F_1 of 0.76.

6 Contribution

This paper makes three contributions. First, we proposed a more appropriate definition for *character* in narrative, in contrast to prior computational works which did not provide a theoretically grounded definition.

Second, we singly annotated 46 Russian folktales and 94 InScript stories for character. The InScript stories are unfortunately not as interesting because they contained only a single protagonist each, only ever referred to in the first person.

Finally, we have demonstrated a supervised machine learning classifier for identifying characters, achieving performance of 0.81 F_1, which shows that the task is feasible but allows for further improvement.

Acknowledgments

This work was supported by NSF CAREER Award IIS-1749917. We would also like to thank the members of the FIU Cognac Lab for their discussions and assistance.

References

David Bamman, Ted Underwood, and Noah A Smith. 2014. A Bayesian mixed effects model of literary character. In *the 52nd Annual Meeting of the Association for Computational Linguistics (ACL)*, pages 370–379, Baltimore, MD.

Ricardo A Calix, Leili Javadpout, Mehdi Khazaeli, and Gerald M Knapp. 2013. Automatic detection of nominal entities in speech for enriched content search. In *Proceeedings of the 26th International Florida Artificial Intelligence Research Society Conference (FLAIRS)*, pages 190–195, St. Pete Beach, FL.

Chih-Chung Chang and Chih-Jen Lin. 2011. LIBSVM: A library for support vector machines. *ACM Transactions on Intelligent Systems and Technology (TIST)*, 2(3):27.

Seymour Chatman. 1986. *Story and Discourse: Narrative Structure in Fiction and Film.* Cornell University Press, Ithaca, NY.

Jacob Cohen. 1960. A coefficient of agreement for nominal scales. *Educational and Psychological Measurement*, 20(1):37–46.

Thierry Declerck, Nikolina Koleva, and Hans-Ulrich Krieger. 2012. Ontology-based incremental annotation of characters in folktales. In *the 6th Workshop on Language Technology for Cultural Heritage, Social Sciences, and Humanities (LaTeCH)*, pages 30–34, Avignon, France.

Joshua Eisenberg and Mark Finlayson. 2017. A simpler and more generalizable story detector using verb and character features. In *the 2017 Conference on Empirical Methods in Natural Language Processing (EMNLP)*, pages 2708–2715, Copenhagen, Denmark.

Mark A. Finlayson. 2008. Collecting semantics in the wild: The story workbench. In *the AAAI Fall Symposium on Naturally Inspired Artificial Intelligence*, pages 46–53. Arlington, VA.

Mark A. Finlayson. 2011. The Story Workbench: An extensible semi-automatic text annotation tool. In *the 4th Workshop on Intelligent Narrative Technologies (INT4)*, pages 21–24. Stanford, CA.

Mark A. Finlayson. 2017. ProppLearner: Deeply Annotating a Corpus of Russian Folktales to Enable the Machine Learning of a Russian Formalist Theory. *Digital Scholarship in the Humanities*, 32(2):284–300.

Monika Fludernik. 2009. *An Introduction to Narratology.* Routledge, New York.

Hui-Ngo Goh, Lay-Ki Soon, and Su-Cheng Haw. 2012. Automatic identification of protagonist in fairy tales using verbs. In *the 15th Pacific-Asia Conference on Knowledge Discovery and Data Mining (PAKDD)*, pages 395–406, Kuala Lumpur, Malaysia.

Labiba Jahan, Geeticka Chauhan, and Mark Finlayson. 2018. A new approach to animacy detection. In *the 27th International Conference on Computational Linguistics (COLING)*, pages 1–12, Santa Fe, NM.

Daniel Jurafsky and James H. Martin. 2007. *Speech and Language Processing*. Prentice-Hall, Englewood Cliffs, NJ.

Nuno Mamede and Pedro Chaleira. 2004. Character identification in children stories. In *The 4th International Conference on Natural Language Processing in Spain (EsTAL)*, pages 82–90, Alicante, Spain.

Christopher D. Manning, Mihai Surdeanu, John Bauer, Jenny Finkel, Steven J. Bethard, and David McClosky. 2014. The Stanford CoreNLP natural language processing toolkit. In *the 52nd Annual Meeting of the Association for Computational Linguistics (ACL): System Demonstrations*, pages 55–60. Baltimore, MD.

Ashutosh Modi, Tatjana Anikina, Simon Ostermann, and Manfred Pinkal. 2017. Inscript: Narrative texts annotated with script information. *arXiv preprint arXiv:1703.05260*.

Graham Alexander Sack. 2013. Character Networks for Narrative Generation: Structural Balance Theory and the Emergence of Proto-Narratives. In *the 4th Workshop on Computational Models of Narrative (CMN'13)*, pages 183–197, Hamburg, Germany.

Hardik Vala, David Jurgens, Andrew Piper, and Derek Ruths. 2015. Mr. Bennet, his coachman, and the archbishop walk into a bar but only one of them gets recognized: On the difficulty of detecting characters in literary texts. In *the 2015 Conference on Empirical Methods in Natural Language Processing (EMNLP)*, pages 769–774, Lisbon, Portugal.

Josep Valls-Vargas, Santiago Ontanón, and Jichen Zhu. 2014. Toward automatic character identification in unannotated narrative text. In *the 7th Intelligent Narrative Technologies Workshop (INT7)*, pages 38–44, Milwaukee, WI.

Jason Y Zhang, Alan W Black, and Richard Sproat. 2003. Identifying speakers in children's stories for speech synthesis. In *the 8th European Conference on Speech Communication and Technology (EUROSPEECH)*, pages 2041–2044, Geneva, Switzerland.

Deep Natural Language Understanding of News Text

Jaya Shree,[1] **Emily Liu,**[2] **Andrew S. Gordon,**[1] and **Jerry R. Hobbs**[1]
[1]University of Southern California, Los Angeles CA USA
[2]Duke University, Durham, NC USA
shree@usc.edu, emily.f.liu@duke.edu, gordon@ict.usc.edu, hobbs@isi.edu

Abstract

Early proposals for the deep understanding of natural language text advocated an approach of "interpretation as abduction," where the meaning of a text was derived as an explanation that logically entailed the input words, given a knowledge base of lexical and commonsense axioms. While most subsequent NLP research has instead pursued statistical and data-driven methods, the approach of interpretation as abduction has seen steady advancements in both theory and software implementations. In this paper, we summarize advances in deriving the logical form of the text, encoding commonsense knowledge, and technologies for scalable abductive reasoning. We then explore the application of these advancements to the deep understanding of a paragraph of news text, where the subtle meaning of words and phrases are resolved by backward chaining on a knowledge base of 80 hand-authored axioms.

Introduction

Typical natural language applications today do an excellent job of performing relatively shallow tasks, such as determining whether a text expresses a predominantly positive or negative sentiment, or doing a fairly direct translation of a string from one language to another. But when people read a text, they construct a much richer model of it than is evident in the output of these applications. In the project described in this paper, we have attempted to explicate all the inferences that people draw in comprehending one 4-sentence, 75-word paragraph from business news, encode the necessary knowledge in first-order logic, and then use an abductive theorem-prover to identify the correct interpretation for the entire paragraph. The knowledge base we constructed for this task consisted of only those axioms needed for the target interpretation, but were written in a general style that did not cater to the requirements of this specific text. Our goal was to explore the scope of the axioms that were required, and to determine whether we could derive the correct interpretation of the whole paragraph using recent advances in incremental abductive reasoning.

The paragraph we used for this exploration was as follows:

> Uber's innovations reflect the changing ways companies are managing workers amid the rise of the freelance-based "gig economy." Its drivers are officially independent business owners rather than traditional employees with set schedules. This allows Uber to minimize labor costs, but means it cannot compel drivers to show up at a specific place and time. And this lack of control can wreak havoc on a service whose goal is to seamlessly transport passengers whenever and wherever they want.

Among the problems this text poses are the following:

1. What are the relations between Uber and "companies", and between "innovations" and "changing ways", as indicated by the verb "reflect"? What does "reflect" mean here?
2. What causal information is provided by the preposition "amid"?
3. What is the relation between gigs and the economy in "gig economy" and how does that relate to "freelance-based"?
4. What are the relations among "workers", "drivers", "employees", and "labor"?

Proceedings of the First Workshop on Narrative Understanding, pages 19–27
Minneapolis, Minnesota, June 7, 2019.

5. What are the relations among "managing workers", "independent", "set schedules", "cannot compel", and "lack of control"?

6. What are the relations among "schedules", "a specific place and time" and "whenever and wherever"?

7. Can we automatically recognize the discourse structure of this paragraph? That is, can we verify the contrast relation between the two clauses of Sentence 3, the causal relation between Sentence 2 and Sentence 3, and the causal relation between Sentences 2-3 and Sentence 4?

8. In the first sentence of the next paragraph there is the referring expression "this fundamental problem". Can we resolve this to Uber's lack of control of its workers? Why is the lack of control a problem?

In this project we were able to address all these problems and enhance the abductive theorem-prover to the point where the proof graph it produced correctly encoded the answers to all these questions. Obviously scaling up will require much more knowledge and more ways of dealing with the combinatorial explosion that this will trigger. But this small-scale exploration has already led to solutions to significant problems and points the way toward larger-scale experiments.

Interpretation as Abduction

Hobbs et al. (1993) presented an approach to language interpretation that rooted in the logical reasoning approach of abduction, or inference to the best explanation. The approach, *interpretation as abduction*, provided an integrated account of syntax, semantics, and pragmatics as a type of search problem, where the aim was to find a set of assumptions that would logically entail the observable words of a text, given a knowledge base of linguistic and commonsense axioms. Among the worked-out examples provided in this paper, the interpretation of a short sentence ("The Boston office called.") is disambiguated by assuming unmentioned entities and relations that connect the words to our commonsense understanding of the world (a person in the office located in Boston made the call). Given sufficiently rich knowledge bases, logical abduction produces many candidate solutions, necessitating a means of favoring some interpretations over others. Here Hobbs et al. describe a scheme of *weighted abduction*, implemented in the TACITUS system, where literals in knowledge base axioms are annotated with numerical weights that transfer and scale costs associated with the input text to terms in the solutions, where the least-cost set of assumptions becomes the preferred interpretation.

Although hugely influential at the time, the proposal of Hobbs et al. (1993) left many challenges that needed to be overcome in order to apply the approach to unconstrained natural language text, including:

1. What commonsense knowledge is necessary, and how should it be obtained?

2. How should knowledge base axioms be annotated with weights?

3. What algorithm would allow logical abduction to scale to large documents and knowledge bases?

In the decades since the publication of this early work, research in natural language processing has followed a radically difference course, beginning first with the data-driven approaches of statistical NLP, leading then to contemporary deep learning approaches that treat syntax, semantics, and pragmatics as implicit, latent encodings of neural network activations. Despite these changing trends, the intervening years has seen enormous progress on addressing the three challenges listed above.

Parsing the Logical Form of the Text

Hobbs et al.'s (1993) proposal viewed the problem of syntax as the conversion of a sequence of words into the *logical form of the text*, where individual morphemes in the text were reified as literals whose arguments encoded their syntactic relationship to other elements, following Hobbs (1985). In their original proposal, this form was abductively derived via a knowledge base of syntactic axioms. However, the emergence of high-accuracy statistical parsers makes this a less than optimal approach to syntactic analysis.

Beginning first with systems that generated the logical form of the text from constituency parsers (Rathod, 2005), recent interpretation pipelines have opted to generate these forms using the output of English Slot Grammar parsers, Combinatory Categorical Grammar parsers, or syntactic dependency parsers, e.g., (Ovchinnikova et al., 2014b,a).

In the current exploration we first used the Boxer system (Bos, 2008) to parse the text and translate it into logical form. This achieved about 80% accuracy, where the two types of mistakes were the usual attachment ambiguities and misalignments between Boxer's output and the logical representation we required. Fixing the latter would have been tedious and unenlightening, and the former was one class of problems we expected to solve with inferencing. So for the rest of this exploration we began with a manually constructed logical form for the text. This enabled us to focus on the less well-understood issues around semantics and pragmatics.

Encodings of Commonsense Knowledge

Spurred by promising results on open-domain question-answering (Moldovan et al., 2003), recent interpretation pipelines have relied on broad-coverage knowledge bases of axioms derived from lexical resources, e.g., using the relations and the glosses in WordNet (Fellbaum, 1998). Ovchinnikova (2012) typifies this approach, where axioms automatically derived from lexical resources are used in abductive reasoning applied to the tasks of recognizing textual entailment, semantic role labeling, and the interpretation of noun dependencies.

Complementing these automatically-derived approaches has been continued progress on the large-scale manual formalization of commonsense knowledge, most notably in the area of commonsense psychology (Gordon and Hobbs, 2017). While the hand-authoring of commonsense domain theories affords a certain level of precision that is not readily obtained using automatic methods, it requires an additional set of so-called *lexical axioms* to bridge the semantic gap between words and the literals used these theories. Montazeri (2014) demonstrates how many of these lexical axioms can be semi-automatically derived by annotating smaller sets of words from large-scale lexical resources.

Probability-ordered Abduction

A frequent critique of Hobbs et al.'s (1993) proposal for weighted abduction was that the weights assigned to knowledge base literals seem arbitrary, lacking a connection to more commonly used numerics such as probability. Indeed, Ovchinnikova et al. (2013) showed that the weights used in weighted abduction cannot be interpreted as probabilities. These concerns have led several researchers to pursue different abductive reasoning frameworks that are more solidly grounded in probability theory, e.g., Blythe et al's. (2011) and Kate and Mooney's (2009) implementations of abduction using Markov Logic Networks.

A more recent advance has been Gordon's (2016) Etcetera Abduction, which builds on earlier work by Poole (1991) on estimating the probability of solutions in Horn-clause abduction. Gordon noted that these solutions could be expressed as conjunctions of so-called *etcetera literals* that reified the uncertainty in a defeasible axiom, following Hobbs et al's (1993) variant of McCarthy's (1986) $\neg$*abnormal* literal, and showed that their probabilities could be readily interpreted as prior and conditional probabilities.

Scalable Abductive Reasoning

Implementations of abductive reasoning must carefully manage the combinatorial search process in order to process long passages of text with sufficient depth, as naive implementations will fail to scale when presented with more than a handful of words. In recent years, several researchers have explored the application of optimized solvers to abductive reasoning, aiming to find solutions for increasingly larger input texts. Inoue and Inui (2013) describe an approach that formulates a weighted abduction problem as a set of linear equations that can be passed to a contemporary integer linear programming solver. Kazeto et al. (2015) further this approach by pre-estimating the relatedness between predicates, and implement their solution in a robust software library called Phillip[1]. Inoue and Gordon (2017) pursue a similar approach within the framework of Etcetera Abduction.

Although the use of optimized solvers allows for substantially longer input, the combinatorial nature of the search problem ultimately limits the scalability of these approaches. An alternative approach to scalable Etcetera Abduction is pursued in Gordon (2018), in which arbitrarily long input sequences are interpreted incrementally, using the best interpretations of previous segments as contexts for the interpretation of the current input window. Given finite window sizes and a finite

[1] https://github.com/kazeto/phillip

beam of running hypotheses, incremental Etcetera Abduction can fail to find the overall best (most-probable) solution, particularly when supporting evidence appears over long distances in the input stream. However, Gordon demonstrated that even with modest window and beam sizes, the available implementation[2] can find near-optimal solutions for interpretation problems with several dozen input literals.

Interpretation of a Paragraph of News Text

To explore the application of contemporary incremental abductive reasoning engines to the interpretation of naturalistic texts, we attempted to use Gordon's (2018) implementation of incremental Etcetera Abduction to interpret a passage of news text. We chose a paragraph from the New York Times article "How Uber Uses Psychological Tricks to Push Its Drivers' Buttons" by Noam Scheiber, which appeared online on April 2, 2017,[3] (presented in the introduction of this paper). The passage explains how the company has undertaken an extraordinary experiment in behavioral science to subtly entice an independent work force to maximize its growth. It starts with explaining how Uber has changed the ways of managing workforce by making them feel more independent, and then it explains the contrast between how its strategy is good in minimizing labor cost but also bad because it can no longer compel its drivers. Finally, it explains how this lack of control is damaging services provided by Uber, which is the fundamental problem they are trying to solve. Our overall conception of the coherence structure of this passage is depicted in Figure 1.

Our aim in this exploration was to determine if we could hand-author a set of first-order axioms (definite clauses) such that the deep meaning of this passage could be automatically recovered following the "interpretation as abduction" approach.

Logical Form of the Text

We began our exploration by applying a contemporary CCG parser (Bos, 2008) to generate the logical form of the text. After some preliminary work with the resulting output, we judged that the automatically-generated logical form of the text

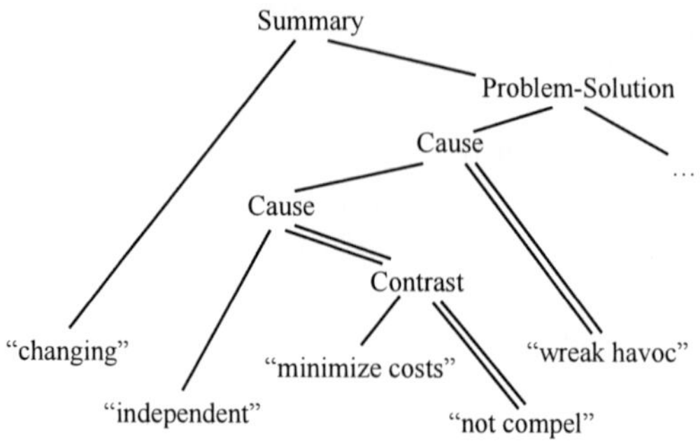

Figure 1: Overall coherence structure of the text

contained too many errors to serve as the starting point for our current investigation. For this reason, we instead opted to hand-author the logical form of the text for each of the four sentences in the passage. The first sentence, "Uber's innovations reflect the changing ways companies are managing workers amid the rise of the freelance-based gig economy," was encoded as follows:

```
(uber u) (poss u x13)
(innovation x13 u x12 x14)
(reflect x13 w11)
(changeIn x15 w11)
(prog x15) (way' e11 w11 e12)
(plural w11 s11)
(company u) (plural u s12)
(manage' e12 u w12) (prog e12)
(pres e12) (workFor w12 u)
(amid w11 r11) (rise r11 x11)
(of r11 x11) (freelance x16)
(base x11 x16) (gig t11 w12 u)
(nn t11 x11) (economy x11)
```

Knowledge Base and Interpretations

To derive the target interpretation for this text passage, we hand-authored a set of 80 axioms (definite clauses) consisting of only those needed as part of the abductive proof structure. While required for this particular text, these axioms were written in a general style so as to better assess the feasibility of the approach on general textual input. Each axiom was assigned an arbitrary probability, reified as an etcetera literal as required by Etcetera Abduction, which will become more relevant as the size of the knowledge base increases. The following are two examples of 80 axioms authored during the course of this exploration.

```
;; failure of u to control is bad for u
(if (and (cannot' e35 e37)
```

[2] https://github.com/asgordon/EtcAbductionPy

[3] https://www.nytimes.com/interactive/2017/04/02/technology/uber-drivers-psychological-tricks.html

```
        (control' e37 u d)
        (etc1_badFor 0.9 e35 u))
    (badFor e35 u))

;; meaning of allow
(if (and (causallyInvolved e31 e32 e33)
         (etc1_allow' 0.9 e31 e32 e33))
    (allow' e31 e32 e33))
```

The following items, depicted in Figure 2, illustrate the kind of knowledge we encoded and the subtleties of text meaning we are capturing in the proof graphs that represent the interpretations.

Meaning of "reflect"

The word "reflect" in this text has deep semantics that expresses why innovation done by Uber is a reflection of changing ways of managing workers. In general terms, an event reflects another event when the former causes knowing the later (Figure 2a).

Meaning of "amid"

To understand the causal force of the preposition "amid" we see first a change in managing as one instance of a change in the economy, since managing is one task in producing goods and services, which is the sort of activity that economies are made up of. Second, we see a change in a whole defeasibly causing change in its parts. As a by-product of explaining "amid" in this way, we resolve the attachment of "amid" to "changing ways" rather than "reflect", "managing" or "workers" (Figure 2b).

Meaning of "rather than"

"Rather than" indicates a contrast, so the interpretation should say what that contrast is. Owners contrast with employees in that the former are not managed by any company, and employees that are managed with some schedule set by the company they work for (Figure 2c).

Contrast between clauses "minimize cost but cannot compel"

Minimized labor cost is good for Uber. However, the inability to compel drivers to show up at specific schedule is not good for them. This contrast between things that are good and bad for Uber explains the presence of the "but" in the sentence (Figure 2d).

Meaning of "This... means"

The coherence relation between sentence 2 and sentence 3 is the predicate-argument relation where "means" is the predicate and the argument is the drivers' independence in sentence 2. The implicational meaning of "mean" is justified by the implicational relation between independence and lack of control.

Causal relationship between sentences 2, 3, and 4

The occurrence of "wreaking havoc" is due to Uber's lack of control (sentence 4), because they cannot compel drivers (sentence 3, which in turn is caused by drivers being independent, sentence 2). Therefore, there is a causal coherence relationship between "wreaking havoc" and "cannot control" (Figure 2f).

"The fundamental problem"

The first sentence of the paragraph that follows this one contains the referring expression "this fundamental problem". We are able to resolve its referent as follows: the lack of control causes damage to the transportation services provided by Uber, which is bad for Uber because it is not able to achieve its goal. And hence, this damage to the service is the fundamental problem for Uber (Figure 2f).

Figure 2 shows how the axioms in our knowledge base resolve each of the challenges listed above, where each of the six graphs are subgraphs of the final interpretation derived for this paragraph of news text.

Over-unification of Literals

In using incremental Etcetera Abduction to derive the target interpretation for this paragraph, we encountered problems that required changes to the available implementation of the reasoning algorithm.

The principal problem we faced was the over-merging of assumptions. In the abductive framework most coreference problems are resolved by inferring implicit redundancies from different parts of the text. That is, entities are identified with each other because they share a property. The difficulty is that if not carefully controlled, this process can identify entities that are not coreferential. We implemented two heuristics that virtually eliminated this problem.

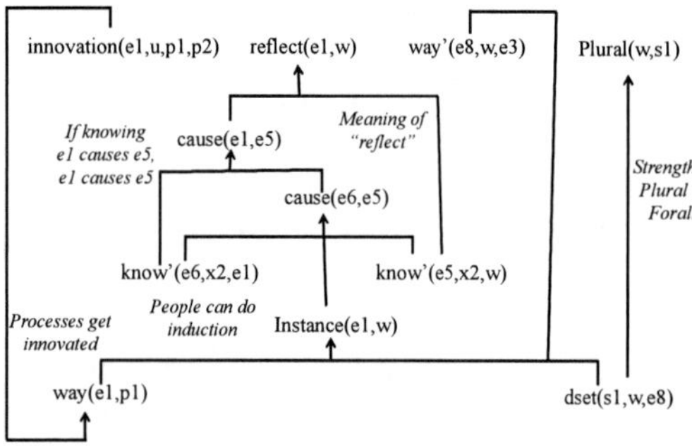

a) innovations **reflect** the changing ways

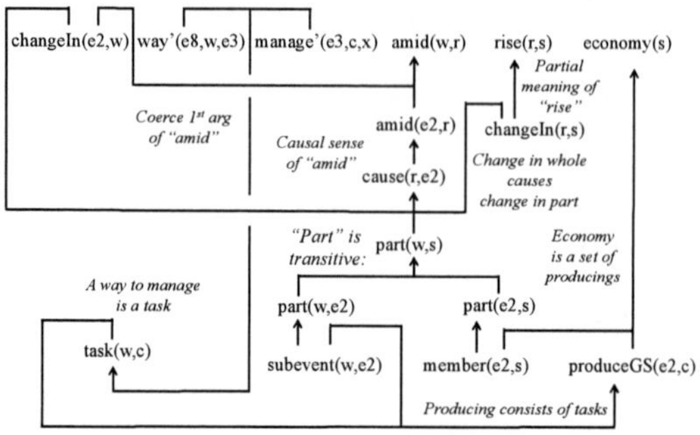

b) changing ways…managing…**amid** the rise of the…economy

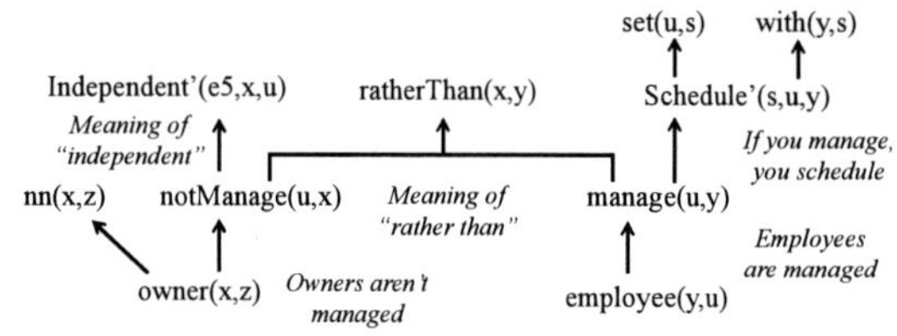

c) independent business owners **rather than** traditional employees with set schedules

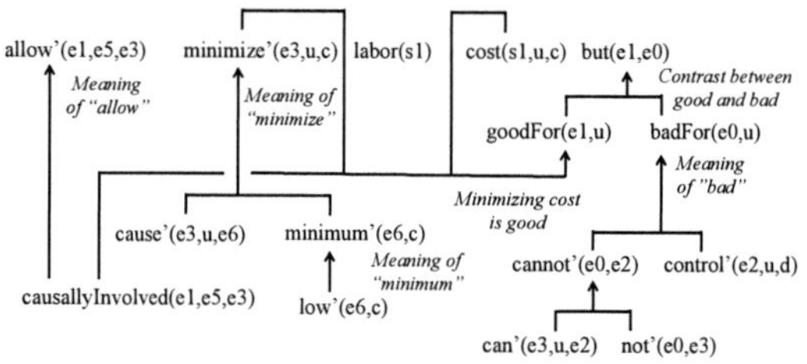

d) allows Uber to **minimize** labor **costs**, **but** means

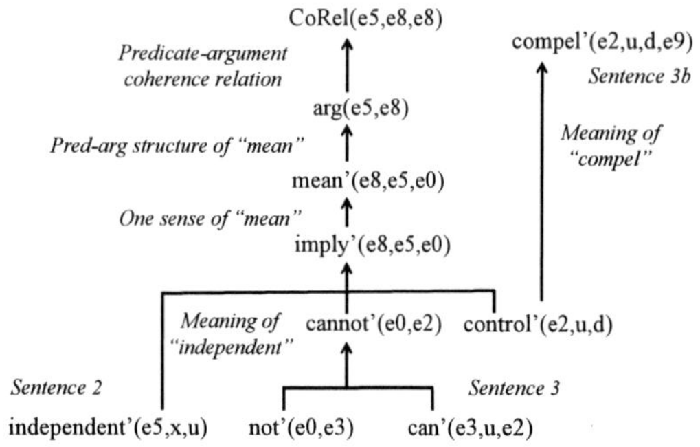

e) independent business owners…**This**..**means** that it cannot compel

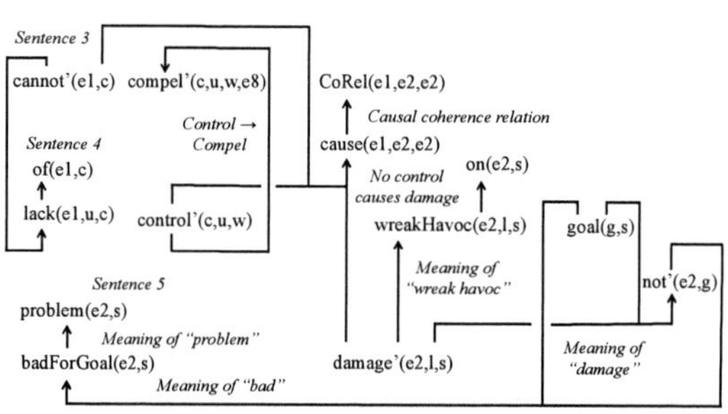

f) cannot compel drivers…lack of control can **wreak havoc** on a service whose goal…solve this fundamental problem…

Figure 2: Six examples of coherence relationships in a paragraph of news text

The first heuristic was this: Suppose we knows $animal(x)$, $animal(y)$, $dog(x)$ and $cat(y)$. Should we identify x and y on the basis of their both being animals? Obviously not, because they have other, contradictory properties—dog and cat. The general rule schema underlying this heuristic is

$$p(\ldots, x, \ldots) \wedge q(\ldots, x, \ldots) \rightarrow \perp$$

or equivalently,

$$p(\ldots, x, \ldots) \wedge q(\ldots, y, \ldots) \rightarrow x \neq y$$

We implemented this class of constraints efficiently in terms of bit matrices.

An example of the second class of constraints is that something cannot be a part of itself. That is, you can't have $part(x, x)$. The general rule schema for this heuristic is

$$p(\ldots, x, \ldots, x, \ldots) \rightarrow \perp$$

or equivalently,

$$p(\ldots, x, \ldots, y, \ldots) \rightarrow x \neq y$$

The two heuristics together blocked every illegitimate case of merging in our data, while letting the correct ones through. As a side-effect of this, it greatly speeded up processing.

Depth, Window, and Beam Parameters

At the beginning of our efforts, we attempted to use Gordon's original implementation of Etcetera Abduction (Gordon, 2016) to interpret each sentence individually, but found that the the size of the input was too great, leading to a combinatorial explosion in the search space. We subsequently used the implementation of incremental Etcetera Abduction (Gordon, 2018), treating the entire paragraph as a single input sequence, ignoring sentence boundaries. To achieve our target interpretations, we modified the software to prevent existentially quantified variables from being turned into constants after each increment of the interpretation process.

Using our hand-authored knowledge base of 80 axioms, we were able to achieve our target interpretation of this text using the modified version of incremental Etcetera Abduction. We found that this interpretation could be found using a modest window parameter of only four literals, and a very small beam of two running hypotheses. However, a large depth parameter of seven backward-chaining steps was required given our formalization of the requisite semantic knowledge, which is substantially larger than required for previous non-linguistic interpretation problems (Gordon, 2016, 2018). The final abductive proof graph consisted of 32 assumptions of prior probabilities and 71 assumptions of conditional probabilities in order to logically entail the logical form of this passage of text given our knowledge base.

Conclusions

In the end we were able to run the entire 75-word paragraph and produce the correct interpretation (proof graph). No incorrect identifications of entities were made. This interpretation included the correct coherence structure and the correct resolution of the definite noun phrase "this fundamental problem" to the lack of control referenced several places in the paragraph. Our success in achieving the target interpretation using incremental logical abduction demonstrates that recent technological advances constitute real progress toward practical implementations.

As encouraging as this result is, there are several obvious questions. First, how will it do on the next paragraph, and the next? How large a knowledge base will be needed before previously unseen texts can be processed and understood? How should that knowledge base be constructed? Given that large knowledge base, can the combinatorial explosion be contained for realistically long and complex texts? What further techniques will be required beyond the incremental processing we employed here?

This work does offer insight into how a knowledge base can be devised to best address subtleties that are prevalent in real-world text. About a third of the axioms we encoded were essentially lexical knowledge, of the sort that standard lexical resources can be expected to provide, such as the implicational sense of "means" and the relation between "workers" and "labor". Another third of the axioms were rules we had already encoded in core commonsense theories (Gordon and Hobbs, 2017), such as the transitivity of "part" in the theory of composite entities, and the axiom in the theory of knowledge management that says people can do induction, i.e., draw general conclusions from specific instances. On the other hand, we also had to encode axioms to coerce or shuffle arguments around, such as coercing from a causal relation to the effect, in order to get the predicate-argument relations right. These rules had a very ad hoc feel, and it would be good to develop a more general approach to this class of problems.

Our analysis of this one paragraph also helped gauge the utility of current technologies for identifying the logical form of the text, where we see the need for further improvement. Likewise, our efforts identified a number of problems with the available implementation of incremental Etcetera Abduction, which we addressed by making modifications to this software. Our expectation is that we would have faced these problems regardless of the passage selected for our analysis, and that future analyses of a similar sort would uncover additional problems to address. In this respect, we see a path forward in this line of research that analyzes different and longer passages of text, uncovering and solving new technical problems and further characterizing the scope of the knowledge engineering requirements. As the software architecture becomes more robust and the knowledge base becomes well-understood, efforts can be increasingly directed toward the automatic acquisition of the axioms required for the deep understanding of arbitrary news text.

The results of this exploration have been good enough to encourage us to continue this line of research, but at best, it has so far given us only a partial proof of possibility of abductive interpretation of complex real-world discourse.

Acknowledgments

This work is supported by Contract W911NF-15-1-0543 with the US Defense Advanced Research Projects Agency (DARPA). This research was supported by the Office of Naval Research, grant N00014-16-1-2435.

References

James Blythe, Jerry R. Hobbs, Pedro Domingos, Rohit J. Kate, and Raymond J. Mooney. 2011. Implementing weighted abduction in markov logic. In *Proceedings of the Ninth International Conference on Computational Semantics*, IWCS '11, pages 55–64, Stroudsburg, PA, USA. Association for Computational Linguistics.

Johan Bos. 2008. Wide-coverage semantic analysis with boxer. In *Proceedings of the 2008 Conference on Semantics in Text Processing*, pages 277–286. Association for Computational Linguistics.

Christiane Fellbaum. 1998. *WordNet*. Wiley Online Library.

Andrew S. Gordon. 2016. Commonsense interpretation of triangle behavior. In *Thirtieth AAAI Conference on Artificial Intelligence*, pages 3719–3725, Palo Alto, CA. AAAI Press.

Andrew S. Gordon. 2018. Interpretation of the Heider-Simmel film using incremental etcetera abduction. *Advances in Cognitive Systems*, 6:1–16.

Andrew S. Gordon and Jerry R. Hobbs. 2017. *A formal theory of commonsense psychology: How people think people think*. Cambridge University Press, Cambridge, UK.

Jerry R. Hobbs. 1985. Ontological promiscuity. In *Proceedings of the 23rd Annual Meeting on Association for Computational Linguistics*, pages 60–69. Association for Computational Linguistics.

Jerry R. Hobbs, Mark E. Stickel, Douglas E. Appelt, and Paul Martin. 1993. Interpretation as abduction. *Artificial Intelligence*, 63(1-2):69–142.

Naoya Inoue and Andrew S. Gordon. 2017. A scalable weighted Max-SAT implementation of propositional etcetera abduction. In *Proceedings of the 30th International Conference of the Florida AI Society*, pages 62–67, Palo Alto, CA. AAAI Press.

Naoya Inoue and Kentaro Inui. 2013. Ilp-based inference for cost-based abduction on first-order predicate logic. *Journal of Natural Language Processing*, 20(5):629–656.

Rohit J. Kate and Raymond J. Mooney. 2009. Probabilistic abduction using markov logic networks. In *Proceedings of the IJCAI-09 Workshop on Plan, Activity, and Intent Recognition (PAIR-09)*.

John C. McCarthy. 1986. Applications of circumscription to formalizing common sense knowledge. *Artificial Intelligence*, 28:89–116.

Dan Moldovan, Christine Clark, Sanda Harabagiu, and Steve Maiorano. 2003. Cogex: A logic prover for question answering. In *Proceedings of rthe North American Chapter of the Associateion for Computational Linguistics*.

Niloofar Montazeri. 2014. *Building a Knowledgebase for Deep Lexical Semantics*. Ph.D. thesis, University of Southern California.

Ekaterina Ovchinnikova. 2012. *Integration of World Knowledge for Natural Language Understanding*. Atlantis Press.

Ekaterina Ovchinnikova, Andrew S. Gordon, and Jerry. R. Hobbs. 2013. Abduction for discourse interpretation: A probabilistic framework. In *Proceedings of the Joint Symposium on Semantic Processing*, pages 42–50.

Ekaterina Ovchinnikova, Ross Israel, Suzanne Wertheim, Vladimir Zaytsev, Niloofar Montazeri, and Jerry Hobbs. 2014a. Abductive inference for interpretation of metaphors. In *Proceedings of the Second Workshop on Metaphor in NLP*, pages 33–41.

Ekaterina Ovchinnikova, Niloofar Montazeri, Theodore Alexandrov, Jerry R. Hobbs, Michael C. McCord, and Rutu Mulkar-Mehta. 2014b. Abductive reasoning with a large knowledge base for discourse processing. In H. Hunt, J Bos, and S. Pulman, editors, *Computing Meaning*, volume 4, pages 107–127. Springer.

David Poole. 1991. Representing bayesian networks within probabilistic horn abduction. In *Proceedings of the Seventh Conference on Uncertainty in AI*, pages 271–278.

Nishit Rathod. 2005. LFToolkit. Https://www.isi.edu/ hobbs/ LFToolkit/.

Kazeto Yamamoto, Naoya Inoue, Kentaro Inui, Yuki Arase, and Junı́chi Tsugii. 2015. Boosting the efficiency of first-order abductive reasoning using pre-estimated relatedness between predicates. *International Journal of Machine Learning and Computing*, 5(2):114–120.

Extraction of Message Sequence Charts from Narrative History Text

Girish K. Palshikar Sachin Pawar Sangameshwar Patil
Swapnil Hingmire Nitin Ramrakhiyani Harsimran Bedi
{gk.palshikar,sachin7.p,sangameshwar.patil}@tcs.com
{swapnil.hingmire,nitin.ramrakhiyani,bedi.harsimran}@tcs.com
TRDDC, TCS Research and Innovation, India

Pushpak Bhattacharyya
pb@cse.iitb.ac.in
IIT Patna, India

Vasudeva Varma
vv@iiit.ac.in
IIIT Hyderabad, India

Abstract

In this paper, we advocate the use of Message Sequence Chart (MSC) as a knowledge representation to capture and visualize multi-actor interactions and their temporal ordering. We propose algorithms to automatically extract an MSC from a history narrative. For a given narrative, we first identify verbs which indicate interactions and then use dependency parsing and Semantic Role Labelling based approaches to identify senders (initiating actors) and receivers (other actors involved) for these interaction verbs. As a final step in MSC extraction, we employ a state-of-the art algorithm to temporally re-order these interactions. Our evaluation on multiple publicly available narratives shows improvements over four baselines.

1 Introduction

Narrative texts, particularly in history, contain rich knowledge about actors and interactions among them along with their temporal and spatial details. For such texts, it is often useful to extract and visualize these interactions through a set of inter-related timelines, one for each actor, where the timeline of an actor specifies the temporal order of interactions in which that actor has participated. *Message Sequence Chart (MSC)* is an intuitive visual notation with rigorous mathematical semantics that can help to precisely represent and analyze (Alur et al., 1996) such scenarios. Feijs (2000), and Li (2000) propose techniques to convert software requirements to MSC. Event timeline construction is a related task about inferring the temporal ordering among events, but where events are not necessarily interactions among actors (Do et al., 2012). Another related line of research is storyline or plot generation from narrative texts such as news stories or fiction (Chambers and Jurafsky, 2009; Vossen et al., 2015, 2016; Goyal et al., 2010; Kim et al., 2018), which uses different narratological output representations (not MSC), such as event sequences or story curves.

In this paper, we extract actors and their interactions from the given input history narrative text, and map them to actors and messages in the basic MSC notation. We generalize the previous work along several dimensions, and propose an *unsupervised* approach enriched with linguistic knowledge. MSC extracted from the given history text can be analyzed for consistency, similarity, causality and used for applications such as question-answering. For example, from the example in Table 1 we extract the MSC as shown in Figure 1, which can be used to answer questions like `"Whom did Napoleon defend the National Convention from?"`. To the best of our knowledge, this is the first work that uses MSC to represent knowledge about actors and their interactions in narrative history text. Our approach is general, and can represent interactions among actors in any narrative text (e.g., news, fiction and screenplays). We propose unsupervised approaches using dependency parsing and Semantic Role Labelling for extracting interactions and corresponding senders/receivers. We use a state-of-the-art tense based technique (Laparra et al., 2015) to temporally order the interactions to create the MSC.

2 Problem Definition

The input is a document D containing narrative text, and the desired output is an MSC depicting the interactions among the actors. No information about the actors or interactions is given as input; they need to be identified. For history narratives, we define an *actor* as an entity of type Person, Organization (ORG) or Location (LOC), which actively participates in various interactions

Proceedings of the First Workshop on Narrative Understanding, pages 28–36
Minneapolis, Minnesota, June 7, 2019. ©2019 Association for Computational Linguistics

msc A1 = its army; A2 = royalist rebels; A3 = a military school; A4 = artillery department; A5 = the National Convention; A6 = the new government; A7 = his parents; A8 = the island of Corsica; A9 = Napoleon Bonaparte

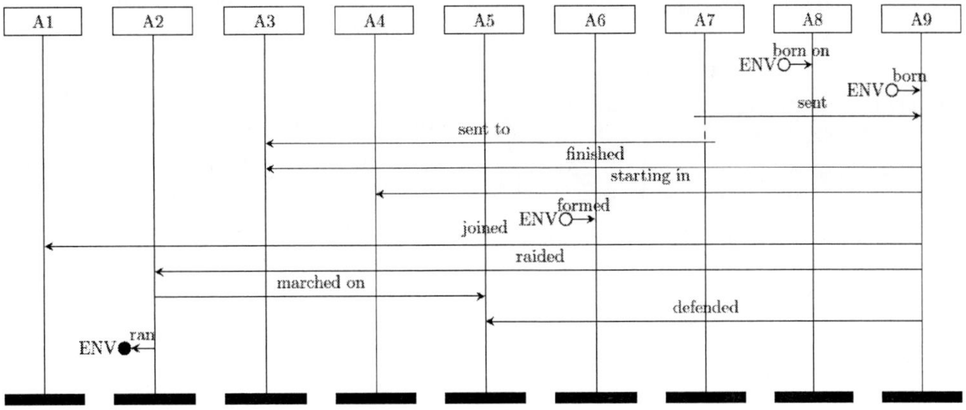

Figure 1: MSC for the example history text.

```
1. Napoleon Bonaparte was born in 1769 on the
island of Corsica.
2. When he was 9 years old, his parents sent him to
a military school.
3. He finished school in 1785 before starting in
the artillery department.
4. When the new government was formed , Napoleon
joined its army.
5. When royalist rebels marched on the National
Convention in October 1795,
      the young officer defended it.
6. The rebels then ran away in panic.
7. Three months earlier, Napoleon had raided the
rebels.
```

Table 1: Sample narrative text. Implicit and explicit temporal expressions are underlined.

with other actors. The reason for including LOC entities as actors is that locations are important in history, and a timeline of events at a particular location provides an interesting perspective. Further, we also need to identify all coreferences of an actor and use a *canonical (i.e., a standardized, normalized)* mention for each; e.g., In Table 1, the actor mentions, `Napoleon Bonaparte`, `Napoleon`, `he` and `the young officer` refer to the actor `Napoleon Bonaparte`.

An *interaction* among actors is either (i) any *deliberate (intentional) physical action*, which is typically initiated by one or more actors and the remaining actors involved in it are affected by it in some way (e.g. `attacked`, `joined`), or (ii) *communication*, which results in passing of information or control among them (e.g. `announced`, `talked`).

We focus on interactions involving one or two actors. An interaction with itself involves only one actor; e.g., `the attackers fled`. When more than two actors are involved in an interaction (e.g., `Napoleon's parents sent him to a military school.`), we break it into several pairwise interactions, if possible. On the other hand, if the sender or receiver in an interaction are missing, we use a dummy actor *environment* (denoted by ENV) as the corresponding sender or receiver. For instance, in the sentence `"The rebels ran away in panic"`, there is no explicit receiver. So, as shown in Fig. 1, we use ENV as the receiver for the message, i.e., we create the message `(The rebels; ran; ENV)`.

Since we represent an interaction as a message in an MSC, the direction of the interaction is important. We assume the direction to be from the initiator of the interaction to the actor affected by it. However, some interactions can be directionless; e.g., `met`, `married`. In such cases, we show the subject of the sentence as sender of the message in MSC. Though our notion of an interaction is similar to an event, a key difference between them is that there is explicit and intentional involvement of actors in an interaction; e.g., `an earthquake` is an event but it is not an interaction.

Temporal ordering of messages is the important and culminating step in the overall process of automated MSC extraction from narrative text. We need to exploit temporal clues available in the input narrative text to derive the temporal order among the messages in the MSC.

2.1 Scope

In this paper, we focus on interactions expressed using verbs because most of the action events in a language are expressed using verbs. We consider interactions expressed using nouns as part of future work. Not all interactions in history narratives are important for creating an MSC. E.g., *mental actions*, such as `felt cheated`, `came to know`, `assumed`, `considered`, `envisioned`, are not considered as interactions. Copula verbs and verbs denoting a state of an object or actor also do not trigger an interaction and hence, such verbs are ignored.

3 MSC Extraction

3.1 Actor Identification

We first make one pass through the text and identify all the actors who are involved in one or more interactions. We group all co-referring mentions of an actor into a set, and choose one *canonical mention* as a representative on the MSC. One complication can occur due to *complex actors*, which is an actor that contains multiple actors, one of which is *independent* and the others are *dependent* and serve to elaborate on the independent actor; e.g., `his parents`, `military school`, `the army of the new government`. We need to identify a complex actor as a whole, and not its constituent actors separately. We use the algorithm in (Patil et al., 2018) to identify an actor and all its coreferents.

3.2 Interaction Identification

Typically the input text mentions many different interactions, and identifying each verbal interaction is required, omitting non-interactions as discussed in Section 2.1. A simple algorithm classifies each verb in the given sentence as an *action verb* or a *communication verb* (and ignores other types of verbs) using WordNet hypernyms of the verb itself or its nominal forms. For example, for the verb `defended`, one of its nominal forms, `defence`, has the category **act** in its hypernym tree; so it is classified as an action verb.

Since we are focusing on interactions that have already occurred, we focus on verbs in the past tense. In some cases, a verb not in the past tense, should also be considered as having past tense; e.g., in `Growing up in rural Hunan, Mao described his father as a stern disciplinarian`, "`Growing`" should be considered to be in the past tense. To achieve this, we systematically *propagate* the past tense to other verbs using linguistic rules. To detect verbs in past tense, we traverse the dependency parse tree of the input sentence in breadth-first-search (BFS) manner. A verb having POS tag of *VBD* is definitely in the past tense. A verb with *VBG* or *VBN* POS tag is considered to be in past tense if: (i) it is a child of another verb tagged with *VBD*; or (ii) it is the parent of an auxiliary verb tagged with *VBD*. An infinitive verb is deemed to be in past tense if it has a governor in the dependency tree with dependency relation either **advcl:to** or **xcomp** and the governor is tagged with *VBD*. In the above sentence, `described` is tagged with *VBD* and hence it is in past tense; `Growing` is tagged with *VBG* and is child of `described` in the dependency parse tree; hence, it is also considered to be in the past tense.

3.3 Message Creation

We need to map each identified interaction to one or more messages in the output MSC. We also need to identify the sender (initiator of the interaction) and receiver (other actors involved in the interaction) for each message. We have developed several approaches for identifying a set of senders (SX) and a set of receivers (RX) for each valid interaction verb. If SX and RX are both empty, we ignore that interaction. If only one of them is empty, we add a special actor *Environment* (ENV) to that set. Once such sets are identified, a message is created for each unique combination of a sender and a receiver for a particular interaction verb.

Dependency parsing-based Approaches: We developed two approaches for message creation based on dependency parsing output: i) Baseline **B1** which directly maps the dependencies output to messages and ii) Approach **M1** (Algorithm 1) which builds on the dependencies output by applying additional linguistic knowledge. We use Stanford CoreNLP (Manning et al., 2014) for dependency parsing.

Baseline B1 simply maps each interaction verb in the dependency tree to a set of messages. Actors directly connected to an interaction verb with certain dependency relations ($nsubj$, $nmod{:}agent$) are identified as senders whereas actors directly connected to the verb with certain other dependency relations ($dobj$, $nsubjpass$, $xcomp$, $iobj$, $advcl{:}to$, $nmod{:}*$) are identified as receivers.

Approach M1 improves upon this baseline by generalizing connections between the verb and potential senders and receivers. Rather than considering only direct connections in dependency tree, M1 identifies certain actors as senders which are connected to the verb with a set of allowable dependency paths such as $nmod{:}poss \rightarrow nsubj$ or $nsubj \rightarrow advcl$ (lines 3-9 in Algorithm 1). E.g., consider the sentence `Bravery of Rajputs pushed the Mughals back`. Here, `Rajputs` is not directly connected to `pushed` in the dependency tree. Still, M1 would be able to identify `Rajputs` as sender because its dependency path to the verb `pushed` is $nmod{:}of \rightarrow nsubj$. Similarly, M1 identifies certain actors as receivers which are descendants of the verb in the dependency tree and the dependency paths connecting them to the verb satisfy certain properties such as "no other verb is allowed on the path" (lines 10-13 in Algorithm 1). Presence of another intermediate verb on such dependency path is a strong indicator that the receiver is an argument for the intermediate verb. For example, in the sentence `Crossing the Alps, Napoleon attacked Italy.`, "`the Alps`" is not a valid receiver for the verb `attacked` because another verb `Crossing` occurs on the dependency path connecting `the Alps` to `attacked`.

SRL-based Approaches: We developed two approaches for message creation based on SRL: i) Baseline **B2** which directly maps the SRL output to messages and ii) Approach **M2** (Algorithm 2) which builds on the SRL output by applying additional linguistic knowledge. We use MatePlus (Roth and Lapata, 2015) for SRL which produces predicate-argument structures as per PropBank (Kingsbury and Palmer, 2002). The baseline B2 simply maps each verbal predicate corresponding to an interaction verb to a set of messages. Actors corresponding to A0 arguments of a verbal predicate are identified as senders whereas actors corresponding to other arguments are identified as receivers.

Approach M2 improves upon this baseline by using VerbNet (Schuler, 2005) roles (the function *vnrole*) associated with PropBank arguments. Certain selectional preferences are used on these VerbNet roles, so as to qualify them as valid senders or receivers. These preferences are based on the linguistic knowledge and the details are described in the Algorithm 2. E.g., consider the sentence `Peter described John as very polite`. Here, for the communication verb `describe`, $vnrole$ (describe.01.A1) $=$ $theme$. As per our linguistic rule, even if any actor is part of *theme* of a communication verb, that actor does not qualify to be a receiver, as it is not directly participating in the interaction. Line 18 in Algorithm 2 encodes this rule, thereby not allowing any actor which is part of a *theme* to be a receiver. Hence, in this example sentence, `John` will not be a receiver for `describe`.

Algorithm 2 also handles a special case about *Ergative* verbs which lie in between the spectrum of transitive and intransitive verbs. Their most distinguishing property is that when an ergative verb does not have a direct grammatical object, its grammatical subject plays an object-like role. E.g., consider following two sentences containing an ergative verb `move`:
S1: `Mao's father moved him to a hostel.`
S2: `Mao moved to Beijing.`
In S1, `moved` has an object but in S2, it does not have any direct object. Semantic Role Labelling would assign the role A1 (thing moving) to `Mao` in S2 and hence it can not be a sender. But as S2 indicates that the actor (`Mao`) is willingly performing the action of moving, we expect `Mao` to be a sender. Hence, for an ergative verb, even if the SRL assigns A1 role to an actor, we consider such an actor for being sender if no A0 role is assigned for the ergative verb by the SRL (lines 9-13 in Algorithm 2).

Combined SRL and Dependency parsing based Approach (M3): SRL tools are useful to identify senders and receivers of a message, but they do have a few important limitations. E.g. (i) SRL tool may fail to identify any A0 even when it is present or when it assumes the verb does not require A0 in the sentence; (ii) the identified A0 may be wrong or cannot be considered as a sender; (iii) SRL tool may fail to identify any A1/A2 even when it is present; (iv) the identified A1/A2 may be wrong or cannot be considered as a receiver.

We call this combined approach as **M3** which corrects the output of SRL-based approach M2 by using output of the dependencies based approach B1. The intuition, here is that B1 uses only high-precision rules for identifying senders and receivers. Hence, B1's output can be used to correct a few errors introduced in the M2's output. E.g., in `He was accorded a very`

Algorithm 1: *create_messages_M1*

```
input  : s (sentence), A (set of known actors with
         coreferents), v (interaction verb),
         DPOSS = {nmod : poss, nmod : of},
         DS = {nsubj, nmod : agent}, DR =
         {dobj, iobj, nmod*, xcomp, nsubjpass,
         advcl:to}, DI = {advcl:to, xcomp}
output : SX = set of senders, RX = set of receivers
SX, RX := ∅
E_d := GetDependencyTree(s)
  // E_d is set of tuples of the form
     (a, b, dr) where a is governor of b
     with dependency relation dr
foreach actor a ∈ A s.t. a has mention in s do
    if (v, a, ds) ∈ E_d ∧ ds ∈ DS then
        SX := SX ∪ {a} ; continue
    if (v, a, nmod:*with) ∈ E_d then
        SX := SX ∪ {a} ; continue
    if ∃u s.t.(u, v, advcl*) ∈ E_d ∧ (u, a, ds) ∈
      E_d ∧ ds ∈ DS then
        SX := SX ∪ {a} ; continue
    if ∃u s.t.(v, u, ds) ∈ E_d ∧ ds ∈ DS ∧ u.ner =
      OTHER ∧ (u, a, dp) ∈ E_d ∧ dp ∈ DPOSS
      then SX := SX ∪ {a} ; continue
    if ∃b s.t. b ∈ SX ∧ (b, a, nmod:*with) ∈ E_d
      then SX := SX ∪ {a} ; continue
foreach actor b ∈ A \ SX s.t. b has a mention in s and
  ∃ path P from v to b in G using E_d do
    if ∃u ≠ v s.t. u.POS = VB* ∧ u ∈
      P ∧ (v, u, dr) ∈ E_d ∧ dr ∉ DI then
      continue
    if ∃u ≠ v s.t. u.POS = VB* ∧ u ∈
      P ∧ (v, u, *) ∉ E_d then continue
    if ∃x in P s.t.(x, b, dr) ∈ Ed ∧ dr ∈ DR then
        RX := RX ∪ {b}
return (SX, RX)
```

Algorithm 2: *create_messages_M2*

```
input : s (sentence), A (set of known actors with
        coreferents), v (interaction verb),
        B_0 = {agent, theme, cause},
        B_1 = {experiencer},
        B_2 = {AMLOC, AMDIR},
        B_3 = {asset, cause, extent, instrument,
        stimulus, time, topic, theme, predicate},
        B_4 = {theme}, B_5 = {agent, theme}
output: SX = set of senders, RX = set of receivers
H := MatePlus(S); // output of MatePlus
SX, RX := ∅;
if v ∉ H ∨ is_copula_like(v) then return(SX, RX)
if H.v has argument A_0 then
    x := H.v.A_0.phrase;
    if x contains an actor from A then
        if vnrole(H.v.A_0) ∈ B_0 ∨ (is_comm(H.v) ∧
          vnrole(H.v.A_0) ∈ B_1) then
            SX := SX ∪ {get_actor(x, A)};
else if is_ergative(v) ∧ H.v has argument A_1 then
    x := H.v.A_1.phrase;
    if x contains an actor from A then
        if vnrole(H.v.A_1) ∈ B_5 then
            SX := SX ∪ {get_actor(x, A)};
foreach argument A_i (i > 0) in H.v do
    x := H.v.A_i.phrase;
    if x contains no actor from A \ SX then continue

    if H.v.A_i ∈ B_2 ∨ vnrole(H.v.A_i) ∉
      B_3 ∨ (is_action(H.v) ∧ H.v.A_i ∈ B_4) then
        RX := RX ∪ {get_actor(x, A)};
if H.v has another predicate v' as argument then
    SX', RX' := create_messages_M2(S, A, v');
    RX := RX ∪ RX';
return(SX, RX)
```

`cordial reception and was loaded with gifts.`, MatePlus (in M2) identifies `He` as A0 for `accorded`, which is wrong because `He` is not the initiator of this interation; `He` should be A1 for `accord`. We correct this by using the fact that B1 (dependencies based approach) detects the **nsubjpass** dependency between `accorded` and `He` and identifies `He` as receiver. As another example, for `His father united him in an arranged marriage to Luo Yigu, thereby uniting their land-owning families.`, MatePlus does not identify any A0 for `uniting`, where the true A0 is `His father`, which we correct using the dependency parse in which `His father` is connected to `uniting` through the path $nsubj \rightarrow advcl$.

3.4 Message Label Generation

We propose a simple algorithm for generating a clear and intuitive label for each message, covering various scenarios. For a verbal event, the label includes the main verb (`joined`), followed by a particle if present (`set_up`), a preposition if present (`cut_off_from`), a negation if present (`not_cut_off_from`), a secondary verb if present (infinitive, gerund or past participle), which also may be followed by a particle and/or preposition (`set_up_to_defend`, `helped_organize`, `set_up_for_taking_away_from`). The general syntax of our message label is given by the regex: `NEG? MAIN_VERB PARTICLE? (PREP|to)? (NEG? SECONDARY_VERB PARTICLE? PREP?)?`. We do not include adverbs, nor any nominal objects and arguments as part of the message label. We also do not include any auxiliary or modal verbs; e.g., from `had fled`, `was elected` we get the message labels `fled`, `elected`. Syntactic verbal structures such as `could have helped` indicate interactions that may not have taken place; so no messages are created for them.

3.5 Temporal Ordering of Messages

Temporal ordering of messages in a MSC is the final step and an important sub-problem of the overall high-level goal of automated MSC extraction. To order the messages, it is important to assign a temporal anchor to each message. A temporal anchor is a point in time (such as `1795-10-01`), at which an interaction has happened. The granularity of the temporal anchor is defined at the level of a year (`1795`), a month (`1795-10`) or a day (`1795-10-01`), but not lower.

We can observe sentences in a narrative which contain explicit time expressions (timex). Explicit timex are date points which are self-contained (e.g., `October 1795`) or can be resolved based on previously occurring dates (e.g., `Three months earlier`). Temporal anchors of messages in such sentences can be assigned normalized values of the explicit timex. To achieve this, we first identify these explicit timex and normalize them using the Heideltime timex recognizer and normalization system (Strötgen and Gertz, 2015). Secondly, the normalized explicit timex is assigned as the temporal anchor of the message which is present in the sentence. In case of sentences with multiple message verbs, the normalized explicit timex is assigned as the temporal anchor of the message which has its main verb nearest to the timex in the sentence's dependency tree.

However, it is important to note that messages may be in sentences without any explicit timex. In order to find the temporal anchor of such messages we employ the "document level time-anchoring (DLT)" algorithm proposed by (Laparra et al., 2015). The algorithm takes a list of messages (as per the text order) and document creation time (DCT) as inputs. The key assumption behind the algorithm is that all the messages of exactly same tense tend to occur in the text order, unless stated explicitly. In other words, the author will mention an explicit timex for the current message with tense t, only if its temporal anchor is different from the anchor of the last message of tense t.

The algorithm proceeds as follows: If a message m has a time anchor t obtained from an explicit timex, then t is stored in a tense-to-anchor map as the last seen anchor associated with the tense of m. However, if m does not have a temporal anchor assigned, then the last seen anchor of the message's tense is obtained from the tense-to-anchor map and set as m's temporal anchor. If the tense-to-anchor map does not have a mapping for m's tense then the provided DCT is set as m's temporal anchor.

Once all messages are assigned some temporal anchor, a simple sorting algorithm is used to order the messages based on their anchors. While sorting it is taken care that the assumption of *ordering messages with the same temporal anchor by their text order* is maintained.

4 Experimental Evaluation

4.1 Datasets

We evaluate our approach on history narratives as they are replete with multiple actors, spatio-temporal details and have varied forms of interactions. We choose public narratives of varying linguistic complexity to cover a spectrum of history: (i) famous personalities: Napoleon (**Nap**) (Littel, 2008), and Mao Zedong (**Mao**) (Wikipedia, 2018), (ii) a key event: Battle of Haldighati (**BoH**) (Chandra, 2007), and (iii) a major phenomenon: Fascism (**Fas**) (Littel, 2008).

We also use a subset of the Facebook's bAbI QA dataset (Weston et al., 2015) which is a text understanding and reasoning benchmark. Our **bAbI** dataset includes 10 instances from the time-reasoning subset of the bAbI QA dataset. Each instance consists of two interleaved sets of information: a set of sentences describing an event and its time for e.g. `Mary went to the cinema yesterday.`, and a set of temporal reasoning questions which need to be answered based on the sentences seen till that instant. We remove the questions from each instance keeping only the event description sentences as input to the approach.

We manually annotated these datasets for independent actor mentions, their aliases (canonical mentions), interaction verbs, complete messages and temporal ordering of the messages. Number of sentences and messages for the datasets are: Nap (106, 99), Fas (117, 115), BoH (77, 133), Mao (58, 135) and bAbI (118, 118).

4.2 Evaluation

We give highest priority to the message label and hence senders / receivers of a message are deemed to be correct only if the corresponding message label has been identified correctly. As one of the evaluation measures, we report the F-measure for identifying only the message labels, ignoring the corresponding senders / receivers.

We further evaluate message identification performance of the proposed approaches at two levels: i) complete messages with actor mentions (denoted as L_1 level) and ii) complete messages with canonical mentions of the actors (L_2 level). As described in Section 3.1, each actor mention has a canonical mention associated with it, which represents a group of corefering actor mentions. At L_1 level, a predicted message is counted as a true positive if the combination of the predicted sender mention, receiver mention and message label (i.e., the complete message) is present in the gold-standard messages for the same sentence. False positives and false negatives are computed on similar lines and overall F-measures are computed for identifying complete messages, at the actor mention level. Similarly, the corresponding F-measures at L_2 (canonical mention) level are also computed by considering canonical senders / receivers instead of their mentions.

We conduct the experiments in two different settings: i) Setting S_1: using gold-standard information about actor mentions, canonical mentions and interaction verbs ii) Setting S_2: using predicted actors and interaction verbs. We use the approach proposed by Patil et al. (2018) for predicting actor mentions and identifying canonical mentions; and a simple algorithm for predicting interaction verbs. For evaluating our temporal ordering approach, we use Kendall's τ rank correlation coefficient (Kendall, 1938) to compare predicted and gold time-lines of a key actor in each dataset (e.g., `Mao Zedong` in the **Mao** dataset).

As goal of Kof's work (Kof, 2007) is same as our work on message extraction, we use it as one of the baselines (B-Kof). We also use OpenIE (Mausam et al., 2012) as another baseline (B-OIE). To avoid unnecessarily penalizing B-OIE, we consider only those extractions where relations fit our definition of interaction verbs and arguments fit our definition of actors. We compare our temporal ordering approach with the default text order based baseline (Text-Order). Table 2 shows comparative performance of the proposed approaches for message extraction and temporal ordering.

4.3 Analysis of Results

It can be observed in Table 2 that our proposed approaches M1 and M2 are consistently outperforming their corresponding baselines for all datasets in Setting S_1. Also, the approach M3 outperforms all other approaches in Setting S_1 when considering actor mentions for the complete message.

F1-measures in the setting S_2 get reduced considerably as compared to S_1. Our approach is a pipeline-based approach where output of actor and interaction verb identification are provided as input for the message creation algorithms. So, the errors in these earlier stages are propagated to the message creation stage, resulting in lower performance for the overall pipeline. Especially, identifying coreferences of actor mentions to determine canonical mentions, is a hard problem (Ng, 2017). Hence, in the setting S_2, we see a significant drop in F1-measure when we go from L_1 level messages to the L_2 level where identification of correct canonical sender / receiver is important.

History narratives tend to describe interactions mostly in the order in which they happen. Hence, we can observe that performance of the DLT based approach and Text-Order baseline is almost similar for the History datasets. In some instances, DLT based approach performs poorly as the default fall back for any previously unobserved tense is the DCT. This can be incorrect if a message with its verb in past_participle is anchored at DCT even after observing multiple previous messages in past tense anchored at an earlier time point. For datasets like bAbI in which text order of interactions differs significantly from the actual temporal order, the performance of the DLT based temporal ordering approach is better than the baseline.

5 Related Work

Though there has been some work in applying MSC for Software Engineering domain, less attention is given to the automatic construction of MSC using NLP. Feijs (2000) proposed an "object-oriented" approach to automatically construct an MSC from a narrative. The approach makes use of a set of generative rules in the form of a grammar. Kof (2007) proposed an approach to construct MSC for modelling scenarios from requirement analysis documents. Kof's approach is based on the situation stack based notion of human attention in a discourse (Grosz et al., 1995). However, the approach makes naive assumptions while finding senders, receivers and action verbs. For example, a sentence contains only one action verb, actors can be found in a pre-defined list and so on. As history narratives include multiple senders/receivers/action verbs and the actors are not pre-specified in a sentence Kof's approach (Kof, 2007) is less suitable.

Our work is close to the work by Chambers and

		Message Label		**Complete Message**				**Temporal Ordering**			
				Actor Mentions		Canonical Mentions		**Text-Order**		**DLT**	
Dataset	**Approach**	S_1	S_2	S_1	S_2	S_1	S_2	S_1	S_2	S_1	S_2
Nap	B-OIE	0.54	0.42	0.38	0.18	0.38	0.18	-	-	-	-
	B-Kof	0.32	0.25	0.17	0.08	0.17	0.08	-	-	-	-
	B1	0.92	0.67	0.49	0.28	0.49	0.32	-	-	-	-
	B2	0.94	0.70	0.64	**0.32**	0.62	**0.34**	-	-	-	-
	M1	**0.95**	0.68	0.51	0.26	0.51	0.31	0.99	0.99	0.95	0.99
	M2	0.94	**0.71**	0.65	0.29	**0.64**	0.29	0.99	0.99	0.99	0.99
	M3	0.94	**0.71**	**0.66**	**0.32**	**0.64**	0.33	0.99	0.99	0.93	0.93
Fas	B-OIE	0.56	0.51	0.44	0.28	0.43	0.19	-	-	-	-
	B-Kof	0.41	0.29	0.22	0.12	0.22	0.07	-	-	-	-
	B1	0.93	**0.63**	0.58	0.31	0.58	0.25	-	-	-	-
	B2	0.92	0.62	0.59	0.29	0.59	0.22	-	-	-	-
	M1	**0.94**	0.60	0.59	0.29	0.59	0.23	0.99	1.0	0.96	0.9
	M2	0.92	**0.63**	0.64	0.28	0.64	0.22	0.99	0.99	0.96	0.89
	M3	0.92	**0.63**	**0.69**	**0.33**	**0.69**	**0.26**	0.97	0.99	0.94	0.89
Mao	B-OIE	0.48	0.50	0.34	0.24	0.35	0.19	-	-	-	-
	B-Kof	0.28	0.29	0.12	0.07	0.12	0.07	-	-	-	-
	B1	0.86	0.72	0.40	0.31	0.41	0.21	-	-	-	-
	B2	**0.93**	0.74	0.61	0.31	0.63	0.18	-	-	-	-
	M1	**0.93**	**0.76**	0.44	0.31	0.45	**0.22**	0.88	0.88	0.84	0.84
	M2	**0.93**	0.73	**0.65**	**0.34**	**0.67**	0.20	0.90	0.88	0.86	0.88
	M3	**0.93**	0.73	**0.65**	0.33	0.66	0.21	0.90	0.88	0.86	0.88
BoH	B-OIE	0.39	0.40	0.28	0.19	0.28	0.04	-	-	-	-
	B-Kof	0.25	0.22	0.09	0.06	0.09	0.02	-	-	-	-
	B1	0.91	0.79	0.58	0.50	0.51	0.21	-	-	-	-
	B2	**0.96**	0.80	0.63	0.43	0.59	0.21	-	-	-	-
	M1	**0.96**	**0.81**	0.64	0.47	0.56	**0.22**	0.96	0.96	0.84	0.81
	M2	**0.96**	0.79	0.65	0.46	0.61	0.21	0.96	0.96	0.84	0.81
	M3	**0.96**	0.79	**0.71**	**0.52**	**0.65**	**0.22**	0.96	0.96	0.84	0.81
bAbI	B-OIE	**1.00**	**1.00**	**1.00**	**0.81**	**1.00**	**0.81**	-	-	-	-
	B-Kof	0.83	0.67	0.83	0.67	0.83	0.67	-	-	-	-
	B1	**1.00**	**1.00**	0.95	0.77	0.95	0.77	-	-	-	-
	B2	**1.00**	**1.00**	0.46	0.39	0.46	0.39	-	-	-	-
	M1	**1.00**	**1.00**	**1.00**	**0.81**	**1.00**	**0.81**	0.73	0.73	1.0	1.0
	M2	**1.00**	**1.00**	**1.00**	**0.81**	**1.00**	**0.81**	0.73	0.73	1.0	1.0
	M3	**1.00**	**1.00**	**1.00**	**0.81**	**1.00**	**0.81**	0.73	0.73	1.0	1.0

Table 2: F1-measures for following approaches- B-OIE: OpenIE baseline, B-Kof: Kof (2007), B1: Baseline using only dependencies, B2: Baseline using only SRL, M1: *create_messages_M1* (Algorithm 1), M2: *create_messages_M2* (Algorithm 2), M3: Combined approach using SRL and dependencies. Setting S_1 corresponds to using gold actors and interaction verbs, Setting S_2 uses predicted actors and interaction verbs

Jurafsky (2009) on modelling of narrative schemas and their participants. They need a *corpus of narratives* to identify prototypical schemas which try to capture common sequence of events. We address a different problem of extracting MSC from a *single* narrative and do not need a corpus. MSC has been proposed as a knowledge representation for a narrative text in (Bedi et al., 2017). We extend their work to automatically construct MSC.

Open Information Extraction (OpenIE) systems aim to extract tuples consisting of relation phrases and their multiple associated argument phrases from an input sentence (Mausam et al., 2012). The predicate-argument structures in OpenIE seem similar to SRL and dependency parsing. However, in dependency parsing the relations are fixed, while SRL systems require deeper semantic analysis of a sentence and hence they depend on lexical resources like PropBank and FrameNet. On the other hand, the predicate-argument structures in OpenIE are not restricted to any pre-specified or fixed list of relations and arguments.

6 Conclusions

Message Sequence Charts (MSC) is an important knowledge representation to summarize and visualize narratives such as historical texts. We proposed algorithms to automatically extract MSC from history narratives. We observed that the state-of-the-art systems of dependency parsing and SRL can not be used as-is for the task. Combining dependency parsing, SRL and linguistic knowledge achieves the best performance on different narratives. We also report results on temporal ordering of messages in the MSC using a tense based temporal anchoring approach.

References

Rajeev Alur, Gerard J Holzmann, and Doron Peled. 1996. An analyzer for message sequence charts. In *International Workshop on Tools and Algorithms for the Construction and Analysis of Systems*, pages 35–48. Springer.

Harsimran Bedi, Sangameshwar Patil, Swapnil Hingmire, and Girish K. Palshikar. 2017. Event Timeline Generation from History Textbooks. In *NLP-TEA@IJCNLP*, pages 69–77.

Nathanael Chambers and Dan Jurafsky. 2009. Unsupervised learning of narrative schemas and their participants. In *Proceedings of the 47th Annual Meeting of the ACL and the 4th IJCNLP of the AFNLP*, pages 602–610.

Satish Chandra. 2007. *Medieval India: From Sultanat to the Mughals- Mughal Empire: Part Two*. Har Anand Publications.

Quang Do, Wei Lu, and Dan Roth. 2012. Joint inference for event timeline construction. In *EMNLP-CoNLL*, pages 677–687.

Loe M. G. Feijs. 2000. Natural language and message sequence chart representation of use cases. *Information & Software Technology*, 42(9):633–647.

Amit Goyal, Ellen Riloff, and Hal Daumé III. 2010. Automatically Producing Plot Unit Representations for Narrative Text. In *EMNLP*, pages 77–86.

Barbara J. Grosz, Scott Weinstein, and Aravind K. Joshi. 1995. Centering: A framework for modeling the local coherence of discourse. *Comput. Linguist.*, 21(2):203–225.

Maurice G Kendall. 1938. A new measure of rank correlation. *Biometrika*, 30(1/2):81–93.

Nam Wook Kim, Benjamin Bach, Hyejin Im, Sasha Schriber, Markus H. Gross, and Hanspeter Pfister. 2018. Visualizing Nonlinear Narratives with Story Curves. *IEEE Trans. Vis. Comput. Graph.*, 24(1):595–604.

Paul Kingsbury and Martha Palmer. 2002. From treebank to propbank. In *LREC*, pages 1989–1993.

Leonid Kof. 2007. Scenarios: Identifying Missing Objects and Actions by Means of Computational Linguistics. In *15th IEEE International Requirements Engineering Conference (RE 2007)*, pages 121–130.

Egoitz Laparra, Itziar Aldabe, and German Rigau. 2015. Document level time-anchoring for timeline extraction. In *ACL (2)*, pages 358–364.

Liwu Li. 2000. Translating use cases to sequence diagrams. In *Proceedings of the 15th IEEE International Conference on Automated Software Engineering (ASE'00)*, page 293.

McDougal Littel. 2008. *World History: Patterns of Interaction*. World History: Patterns of Int. Houghton Mifflin Harcourt Publishing Company.

Christopher D. Manning, Mihai Surdeanu, John Bauer, Jenny Rose Finkel, Steven Bethard, and David McClosky. 2014. The stanford corenlp natural language processing toolkit. In *ACL*, pages 55–60.

Mausam, Michael Schmitz, Stephen Soderland, Robert Bart, and Oren Etzioni. 2012. Open language learning for information extraction. In *EMNLP-CoNLL*, pages 523–534.

Vincent Ng. 2017. Machine learning for entity coreference resolution: A retrospective look at two decades of research. In *AAAI*, pages 4877–4884.

Sangameshwar Patil, Sachin Pawar, Swapnil Hingmire, Girish K. Palshikar, Vasudeva Varma, and Pushpak Bhattacharyya. 2018. Identification of Alias Links among Participants in Narratives. In *ACL*.

Michael Roth and Mirella Lapata. 2015. Context-aware frame-semantic role labeling. *Transactions of the Association for Computational Linguistics*, 3:449–460.

Karin Kipper Schuler. 2005. Verbnet: A broad-coverage, comprehensive verb lexicon.

Jannik Strötgen and Michael Gertz. 2015. A baseline temporal tagger for all languages. In *EMNLP*, pages 541–547.

Piek Vossen, Tommaso Caselli, and Yiota Kontzopoulou. 2015. Storylines for structuring massive streams of news. In *Proceedings of the First Workshop on Computing News Storylines*, pages 40–49.

Piek Vossen, Tommaso Caselli, and Yiota Kontzopoulou. 2016. Storyline detection and tracking using dynamic latent dirichlet allocation. In *Proceedings of 2nd Workshop on Computing News Storylines*, pages 9–19.

Jason Weston, Antoine Bordes, Sumit Chopra, Alexander M Rush, Bart van Merriënboer, Armand Joulin, and Tomas Mikolov. 2015. Towards ai-complete question answering: A set of prerequisite toy tasks. *arXiv preprint arXiv:1502.05698*.

Wikipedia. 2018. Mao zedong — Wikipedia, the free encyclopedia. [Online; accessed 22-Feb-2018].

Unsupervised Hierarchical Story Infilling

Daphne Ippolito*
daphnei@seas.upenn.edu

David Grangier
grangier@google.com

Chris Callison-Burch
ccb@seas.upenn.edu

Douglas Eck
deck@google.com

Abstract

Story infilling involves predicting words to go into a missing span from a story. This challenging task has the potential to transform interactive tools for creative writing. However, state-of-the-art conditional language models have trouble balancing fluency and coherence with novelty and diversity. We address this limitation with a hierarchical model which first selects a set of rare words and then generates text conditioned on that set. By relegating the high entropy task of picking rare words to a word-sampling model, the second-stage model conditioned on those words can achieve high fluency and coherence by searching for likely sentences, without sacrificing diversity.

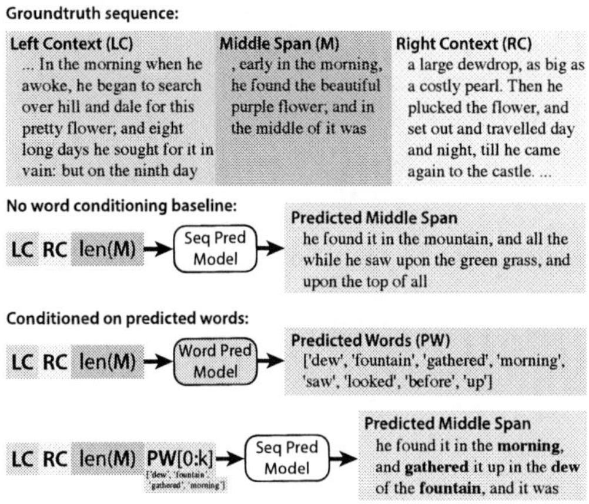

Figure 1: In the one stage baseline, the missing span is predicted given the context and the target length. In the two stage method, words that should go in the span are predicted in inverse frequency order. For visualization, the left and right contexts have been truncated.

1 Introduction

Recent advances in language modeling have made considerable progress towards the automatic generation of fluent text (Jozefowicz et al., 2016; Baevski and Auli, 2019; Radford et al., 2019). This evolution has sparked the development of tools to assist human writers. For instance, Fan et al. (2018b) suggest generating short stories from high-level prompts, Clark et al. (2018b) study the interaction of human and language models for creative writing, and Peng et al. (2018) propose an interactive control of story lines. In addition, products such as Grammarly offer suggestions to improve grammar and wording (Hoover et al., 2015).

Our work is concerned with story infilling. We envision this task as a step towards a suggestion tool to help writers interactively replace text spans. Text infilling, a form of cloze task (Taylor, 1953), involves removing sequences of words from text and asking for a replacement. Compared to traditional left-to-right language modeling, automatic infilling interacts well with human text revision processes, which are rarely purely left-to-right. In the context of story generation, infilling should ensure (i) text fluency, (ii) coherence with the story line, and (iii) text which is not generic or obvious to a human. These three objectives require a delicate balance for modeling since fluency and coherence suggest preferring likely sequences, while novelty suggests preferring less likely sequences.

We observe that recent conditional neural sequence to sequence models (Vaswani et al., 2017) have difficulty with this balance. As a solution, we propose to structure our cloze task in a hierarchical manner. In contrast to Fan et al. (2018b), we do not assume access to a supervised signal describing a hierarchy. We instead decompose our generation task by first randomly sampling from the high entropy part of the signal before generating the lower entropy part conditioned on the former. This decomposition is simple, yet powerful. The first model chooses rare words through ran-

*Work performed while a Google Student Researcher.

Proceedings of the First Workshop on Narrative Understanding, pages 37–43
Minneapolis, Minnesota, June 7, 2019.

dom sampling and the second model then uses a search algorithm to generate likely sequences conditioned on these words. Beam search in the second step allows better fluency (i) and coherence (ii), while conditioning with sampled words prevents novelty (iii) from being compromised.

We evaluate our proposal in the context of infilling passages from children's books and fairy tales. We compare vanilla transformer models with hierarchical alternatives, both through automated metrics and a human study. Our hierarchical method results in greater diversity in the generated text, without sacrificing quality. When we control for diversity, our method strongly outperforms the non-hierarchical baseline.

2 Related Work

Automatic Story Generation Computer-aided story generation has been a source of interest since the early days of NLP. Classical AI algorithms relied on symbolic and logical planning and graph construction (Klein et al., 1973; Meehan, 1977; Turner, 1993; Riedl and Young, 2006). Statistical methods have also been proposed (McIntyre and Lapata, 2009; Li and Riedl, 2015; Gatt and Krahmer, 2018). Recently, the field has been influenced by the success of (conditional) neural language models (Bengio et al., 2003; Schwenk and Gauvain, 2004; Bahdanau et al., 2015; Nallapati et al., 2016). Story generation with neural models include (Chourdakis and Reiss, 2017; Peng et al., 2018; Radford et al., 2019).

We build upon recent work that improves coherence in story generation by using hierarchical neural methods. These approaches allow reasoning at a higher level than words by considering a two-level hierarchy where a structuring representation conditions text generation. Martin et al. (2018) use sequences of events to structure generation while Jain et al. (2017) relies on sequences of short descriptions. Fan et al. (2018b) rely on writing prompts. Closer to our work, Clark et al. (2018a) condition on entity mentions. The training of these methods requires the availability of structuring labels which are either present in the training set (Fan et al., 2018b) or extracted by a separate system (Martin et al., 2018; Clark et al., 2018a). In our case, we avoid this step by considering rare words as the structuring signal.

Infilling Task Rather than generating an entire novel story, our goal is to replace text spans in an existing story to make progress towards interactive assistance for creative writers. Text infilling is known in linguistics as the cloze task (Taylor, 1953) and involves removing words or sequences of words from a text and asking a computer or a human to predict them. Existing work has used the masking of random words to build language models (Fedus et al., 2018) as well as contextualized word embeddings (Collobert et al., 2011; Devlin et al., 2018). Infilling of longer spans has been considered in work that explores bi-directional decoding for image captioning (Sun et al., 2017) .

3 Method

Our method predicts a variable length text span given a fixed length context from either side. We rely on the self-attentive Transformer model (Vaswani et al., 2017) with learned position embeddings, where the encoder takes the context as input and the decoder predicts the missing span. Architecture details and training parameters are in the Appendix. We use the subword tokenizer from (Vaswani et al., 2017), but report all statistics except perplexity in term of proper words. In addition to the context, we also condition our base model on the desired output length. We append to the input sequence a marker token denoting one of 5 possible length bins Fan et al. (2018a). Length conditioning lets us compare different models and decoding strategies with the same average generation length, thus avoiding length preference biases in human evaluation.

In our proposed approach, we decompose the generation task hierarchically, sampling a set of words desired for generation, before generating text that includes these words.

Word Prediction For each infilling instance, our model ingests the context data and predicts a sequence of subwords in frequency order, starting with rare subwords first. The word prediction model is a standard Transformer, for which we prepare the training data such that the target subwords are reordered by increasing frequency.

Our motivation for frequency ordering is twofold. Conceptually, rare words have a denser information content in an information-theoretic sense (Sparck Jones, 1972; Shannon, 1948), i.e., it is easier to predict the presence of common words given nearby rare words than the opposite. Practically, predicting rare words first allows us to interrupt decoding after a fixed number of steps, then

LC	were filled with anger, and decided not to go fishing again, but to wait for the next appearance of the fire. But after many days had passed without their seeing the fire, they went fishing again, and behold, there was the fire!	hand he held an iron club, which he dragged after him with its end on the ground; and, as it trailed along, it tore up a track as deep as the furrow a farmer ploughs with a team of oxen. The horse he	cave, whose mouth is beneath the sea. Here was a broad, dry space with a lofty, salt-icicled roof. The green, translucent sea, as it rolled back and forth at their feet, gave to their brown faces a
GT	And so they were continually tantalized. Only when they were out fishing would the fire appear, and when they	led was even larger in proportion than the giant himself, and quite as ugly. His great carcass was covered all over	ghastly white glare. The scavenger crabs scrambled away over the dank and dripping stones, and the loathsome biting eel, slowly reached
HIER-3	and there was a shout of joy from all the people who went fishing thither, but when they	rode was a lazy ox. He was a very ugly man. He was a man	faint intake of breath, whence it rose and curled, as it were, into the sea. And now it stretched
HIER-max	and thither they gathered together at a strong pace, for it was useless to go fishing at home, and when another shout	was missing stood in lazy work. You could see that he was a big, ugly ox,	shining intake of air, whence the black bear curled up on the surface of the water, and turned its head to look
BASE beam10	and they could not find it. They could not find it, and when the fire was	rode was a man of about thirty-five years of age. He was a tall man,	look of horror and horror. It seemed as if it would burst into a flood, and burst upon them, and burst
BASE sampling10	and the fire, which had been so long gone that many had not been in it for years, and when the fire	had driven was a little man of about the size of a man, with shaggy mane, and	deep, almost awful, impression, like that which was seen on a rock on a rocky beach. But the kangaroo did not stretch
BASE sampling	and at last there was a fierce fire! And at last Rosetta had an arrow, and when Oui	wheeled in without pausing to speak to me was a grotesque specimen of some repulsive animal. He was short of stature,	flood of radiance, sufficient to kill them utterly. [Illustration: It certainly had not a fairy named Serpent] The monster had cast
RC	returned they could not find it. This was the way of it. The curly-tailed alae knew that Maui and Hina had only these four sons, and if any of them stayed on shore to watch the fire while the others were out	with tangled scraggy hair, of a sooty black; you could count his ribs and all the points of his big bones through his hide; his legs were crooked and knotty; his neck was twisted; and as for his jaws, they were	out its well-toothed, wide-gaping jaw to tear the tender feet that roused it from its horrid lair, where the dread sea god dwelt. The poor hapless girl sank down upon this gloomy shore and cried, clinging to the kan

Table 1: Two qualitative examples with context extracted from fairytales. Left context (LC), right context (RC), ground truth center (GT), and the outputs from several methods are shown.

delegate the prediction of more common words to our second-stage model.

Word-Conditioned Generation The second-stage model, also a Transformer, is responsible for generating a text span given the surrounding context, a desired length marker, and a list of words predicted by the first-stage model. It takes as input the concatenation of these three signals.

At training time, we select a list of k words from the missing span to condition on, where k is sampled uniformly between 0 and half the target length. At inference, this model takes conditioning words from the word generation model introduced above. Interestingly, such a word list could be edited interactively by writers, which we defer to future work.

Training with a variable number of conditioning words allows us to choose the number of provided words at inference time. We observe that this choice needs to balance sufficient information to influence coherence and novelty in generated spans, while preserving some headroom for the second stage model to suggest its own common words and produce fluent text. Some examples of the unusual wording choices made when the second stage model is conditioned on all predicted words (HIER-max) can be seen in Table 1.

4 Experiments & Results

Experimental Setup We train on the Toronto Book Corpus (TBC) concatenated with Project Gutenberg, for a total of over 1.2 billion words after filtering our exact duplicate books. We withheld 5% of all books for validation and test.

Training examples consist of a 5 to 50 token-long target sequence, with 50 tokens of context on each side. We experimented with longer context windows but did not observe strong improvement on automated metrics. We do not force any alignment along linguistic boundaries, so context windows and gaps may start or end in the middle of a

Model	Decoding	Diversity		ROUGE-1	PPL	% Votes	p-value
		dist-1	dist-2	F1		against HIER-3	
BASE	beam10	.057	.218	0.29	16.61	48.75	0.82
BASE	sampling10	.058	.304	0.26	16.61	56.67	0.30
BASE	sampling	.101	.477	0.23	16.61	27.78	0.000025
HIER-max	sampling+beam10	.107	.442	0.24	4.22	28.33	0.00079
HIER-3	sampling+beam10	.104	.347	0.27	6.62	–	–

Table 2: Automated and human evaluation for our method (Hier) against baseline (base). Human evaluation reports A/B testing against Hier-3, along with chi-square test p-values.

sentence or even word.

Evaluation Automatic evaluation is performed on 10,000 spans of length 15-30 from our validation set. We report the sub-token perplexity of the reference and evaluate generation diversity with **dist-k**, the total number of distinct k-grams, divided by the total number of tokens produced over all examples in the validation set.

Three children's books were chosen from the validation set for human evaluation (Scott, 1921; Barrow, 1863; Vandercook, 1912). We hoped that the more concise prose in children's literature would make it easier for evaluators to quickly spot mistakes. We selected paragraphs of length 50 to 130 subwords, and randomly replaced a span of 15 to 30 subwords from anywhere in the paragraph.

Human raters were shown two instances of each paragraph, identical except for the selected span, which may have come from one model or another. The modified span was highlighted in each paragraph, and evaluators were asked which highlighted excerpt seemed better (more on-topic, exciting, and/or coherent) given the context. Further details about the task are in the the Appendix.

Results As our motivation is to generate diverse text without compromising on coherence and fluency, we evaluate the baseline non-hierarchical approach at different level of diversity by considering different decoding strategies. Conditional language models generate text word-by-word, either through beam search, i.e. approximating the maximum-a-posteriori sequence (Sutskever et al., 2014), or through sampling. Beam search often leads to repetitive, "safe" outputs, while random sampling results in more diverse outputs that mat suffer from fluency and coherence issues. While some work has incorporated a temperature parameter during random sampling to control the tradeoff between diversity and quality, we instead consider restricting sampling to the top-10 next words (sampling10) (Fan et al., 2018a) as preliminary experiments indicated this method produces higher quality outputs for equivalent levels of diversity.

Table 2 shows that as expected, sampling results in the richest diversity, beam search the poorest, and sampling10 falls between the two. In human evaluation, sampling10 and beam outperform or perform equivalently to our Hier-3 method, but have lower diversity. Unrestricted sampling performs much worse.

In our hierarchical approach (HIER), we achieve both diverse and fluent generation by using random sampling for the word prediction model, where diversity is more critical than fluency, and beam search for the second-stage model.

Table 2 evaluates HIER in two settings, conditioning on all words from the word prediction model or conditioned only on the first three predicted words. Human raters strongly prefer the model conditioned on only three words. We also show that humans rate generation of HIER-3 comparably to BASE/sampling10 while our model achieves much higher diversity (dist-1 and dist-2). Our model therefore achieves its goal of diverse and fluent outputs for story infilling.

5 Conclusions and Future Work

We show that taking a hierarchical approach to story infilling is an effective strategy for balancing fluent and coherent generated text with the diversity and interestingness necessary to build a useful tool for writers. Ultimately, we envision a fully collaborative system, where writers can upload a story and then solicit ideas from the computer on ways to rewrite specific parts. Writers will be able to choose between guiding generation by manually specifying words or concepts to be used, or taking suggestions made by the system.

Future work could investigate insertion-based architectures better suited to the infilling task (Stern et al., 2019), and the use of n-gram phrases instead of independent subwords as conditioning.

References

Alexei Baevski and Michael Auli. 2019. Adaptive input representations for neural language modeling. In *International Conference on Learning Representation (ICLR)*.

Dzmitry Bahdanau, Kyunghyun Cho, and Yoshua Bengio. 2015. Neural machine translation by jointly learning to align and translate. In *International Conference on Learning Representation (ICLR)*.

Fanny Barrow. 1863. *More Mittens: The Doll'S Wedding and Other Stories*. D. Appleton and Company, New York.

Yoshua Bengio, Réjean Ducharme, Pascal Vincent, and Christian Jauvin. 2003. A neural probabilistic language model. *Journal of Machine Learning Research (JMLR)*, 3(Feb):1137–1155.

Emmanouil Theofanis Chourdakis and Joshua Reiss. 2017. Constructing narrative using a generative model and continuous action policies. In *Proceedings of the Workshop on Computational Creativity in Natural Language Generation (CC-NLG 2017)*, pages 38–43.

Elizabeth Clark, Yangfeng Ji, and Noah A Smith. 2018a. Neural text generation in stories using entity representations as context. In *Proceedings of the 2018 Conference of the North American Chapter of the Association for Computational Linguistics: Human Language Technologies, Volume 1 (Long Papers)*, volume 1, pages 2250–2260.

Elizabeth Clark, Anne Spencer Ross, Chenhao Tan, Yangfeng Ji, and Noah A Smith. 2018b. Creative writing with a machine in the loop: Case studies on slogans and stories. In *23rd International Conference on Intelligent User Interfaces*, pages 329–340. ACM.

Ronan Collobert, Jason Weston, Léon Bottou, Michael Karlen, Koray Kavukcuoglu, and Pavel Kuksa. 2011. Natural language processing (almost) from scratch. *Journal of machine learning research*, 12(Aug):2493–2537.

Jacob Devlin, Ming-Wei Chang, Kenton Lee, and Kristina Toutanova. 2018. BERT: pre-training of deep bidirectional transformers for language understanding. *CoRR*, abs/1810.04805.

Angela Fan, David Grangier, and Michael Auli. 2018a. Controllable abstractive summarization. In *Proceedings of the 2nd Workshop on Neural Machine Translation and Generation*, pages 45–54, Melbourne, Australia. Association for Computational Linguistics.

Angela Fan, Mike Lewis, and Yann Dauphin. 2018b. Hierarchical neural story generation. In *Proceedings of the 56th Annual Meeting of the Association for Computational Linguistics (Volume 1: Long Papers)*, pages 889–898, Melbourne, Australia. Association for Computational Linguistics.

William Fedus, Ian Goodfellow, and Andrew Dai. 2018. Maskgan: Better text generation via filling in the ____.

Albert Gatt and Emiel Krahmer. 2018. Survey of the state of the art in natural language generation: Core tasks, applications and evaluation. *Journal of Artificial Intelligence Research*, 61:65–170.

Bradley Hoover, Maksym Lytvyn, and Oleksiy Shevchenko. 2015. Systems and methods for advanced grammar checking. US Patent 9,002,700.

Parag Jain, Priyanka Agrawal, Abhijit Mishra, Mohak Sukhwani, Anirban Laha, and Karthik Sankaranarayanan. 2017. Story generation from sequence of independent short descriptions. In *SIGKDD Workshop on Machine Learning for Creativity (ML4Creativity)*.

Rafal Jozefowicz, Oriol Vinyals, Mike Schuster, Noam Shazeer, and Yonghui Wu. 2016. Exploring the limits of language modeling. *arXiv preprint arXiv:1602.02410*.

Sheldon Klein, John F Aeschlimann, David F Balsiger, Steven L Converse, Mark Foster, Robin Lao, John D Oakley, Joel Smith, et al. 1973. Automatic novel writing: A status report. Technical report, University of Wisconsin-Madison Department of Computer Sciences.

Boyang Li and Mark Riedl. 2015. Scheherazade: Crowd-powered interactive narrative generation. In *Twenty-Ninth AAAI Conference on Artificial Intelligence*.

Lara J Martin, Prithviraj Ammanabrolu, Xinyu Wang, William Hancock, Shruti Singh, Brent Harrison, and Mark O Riedl. 2018. Event representations for automated story generation with deep neural nets. In *Thirty-Second AAAI Conference on Artificial Intelligence*.

Neil McIntyre and Mirella Lapata. 2009. Learning to tell tales: A data-driven approach to story generation. In *Proceedings of the Joint Conference of the 47th Annual Meeting of the ACL and the 4th International Joint Conference on Natural Language Processing of the AFNLP: Volume 1-Volume 1*, pages 217–225. Association for Computational Linguistics.

James R Meehan. 1977. Tale-spin, an interactive program that writes stories. In *International Joint Conference on Artificial Intelligence (IJCAI)*, volume 77, pages 91–98.

Ramesh Nallapati, Bowen Zhou, Caglar Gulcehre, Bing Xiang, et al. 2016. Abstractive text summarization using sequence-to-sequence rnns and beyond. In *Conference on Computational Natural Language Learning (CoNLL)*.

Nanyun Peng, Marjan Ghazvininejad, Jonathan May, and Kevin Knight. 2018. Towards controllable story generation. In *Proceedings of the First Workshop on Storytelling*, pages 43–49.

Alec Radford, Jeffrey Wu Wu, Rewon Child, David Luan Luan, Dario Amodei, and Ilya Sutskever. 2019. Recognizing textual entailment: Rational, evaluation and approaches.

Mark O Riedl and Robert Michael Young. 2006. From linear story generation to branching story graphs. *IEEE Computer Graphics and Applications*, 26(3):23–31.

Holger Schwenk and Jean-Luc Gauvain. 2004. Neural network language models for conversational speech recognition. In *Eighth International Conference on Spoken Language Processing*.

Martin J. Scott. 1921. *A Boy Knight*. P. J. Kenedy & Sons, New York.

Claude Elwood Shannon. 1948. A mathematical theory of communication. *Bell system technical journal*, 27(3):379–423.

Karen Sparck Jones. 1972. A statistical interpretation of term specificity and its application in retrieval. *Journal of documentation*, 28(1):11–21.

Mitchell Stern, William Chan, Jamie Kiros, and Jakob Uszkoreit. 2019. Insertion transformer: Flexible sequence generation via insertion operations. *arXiv preprint arXiv:1902.03249*.

Qing Sun, Stefan Lee, and Dhruv Batra. 2017. Bidirectional beam search: Forward-backward inference in neural sequence models for fill-in-the-blank image captioning. In *Proceedings of the IEEE Conference on Computer Vision and Pattern Recognition*, pages 6961–6969.

Ilya Sutskever, Oriol Vinyals, and Quoc V Le. 2014. Sequence to sequence learning with neural networks. In *Advances in neural information processing systems*, pages 3104–3112.

Wilson L Taylor. 1953. cloze procedure: A new tool for measuring readability. *Journalism Bulletin*, 30(4):415–433.

Scott R. Turner. 1993. *Minstrel: A Computer Model of Creativity and Storytelling*. Ph.D. thesis, Los Angeles, CA, USA. UMI Order no. GAX93-19933.

Margarat Vandercook. 1912. *The Ranch Girls' Pot of Gold*. John C. Winston Company, Philadelphia.

Ashish Vaswani, Samy Bengio, Eugene Brevdo, Francois Chollet, Aidan N. Gomez, Stephan Gouws, Llion Jones, Łukasz Kaiser, Nal Kalchbrenner, Niki Parmar, Ryan Sepassi, Noam Shazeer, and Jakob Uszkoreit. 2018. Tensor2tensor for neural machine translation. *CoRR*, abs/1803.07416.

Ashish Vaswani, Noam Shazeer, Niki Parmar, Jakob Uszkoreit, Llion Jones, Aidan N Gomez, Łukasz Kaiser, and Illia Polosukhin. 2017. Attention is all you need. In *Advances in Neural Information Processing Systems*, pages 5998–6008.

6 Appendix

7 Amazon Mechanical Turk Task

Our evaluation set consisted of 280 paragraphs selected from the evaluation dataset. For each question, evaluators were shown the same paragraph twice, with a highlighted span possibly altered by a model (Figure 2).

In our initial experiments, these questions were split into 20 HITs of 11 questions each. Ten of these questions compared generated text from the two methods of interest, while one other question was a honeypot, where one of the method outputs was replaced by the ground truth. However, after running multiple trial HITs, we found that the task was too hard for the average Turker, and performance on the honeypot question was close to random guessing.

We instead recruited two expert annotators familiar with reading antiquated English and with common language model mistakes to complete the HITs. In total we collected 60+ annotations per comparison task.

8 Model Parameters

All experiments were done with Transformer models implemented in the Tensor2Tensor framework (Vaswani et al., 2018). Important hyperparameters are shown below. All other hyperparameters were left at the Tensor2Tensor default.

```
{
    "attention_dropout": 0.1,
    "batch_size": 4096,
    "dropout": 0.2,
    "ffn_layer": "dense_relu_dense",
    "filter_size": 2048,
    "hidden_size": 512,
    "kernel_height": 3,
    "kernel_width": 1,
    "label_smoothing": 0.0,
    "learning_rate": 0.2,
    "learning_rate_constant": 2.0,
    "learning_rate_decay_rate": 1.0,
    "learning_rate_decay_scheme": "noam",
    "learning_rate_decay_steps": 5000,
    "learning_rate_warmup_steps": 8000,
    "num_heads": 8,
    "num_hidden_layers": 6,
    "optimizer": "Adam",
    "optimizer_adam_beta1": 0.9,
    "optimizer_adam_beta2": 0.997,
```

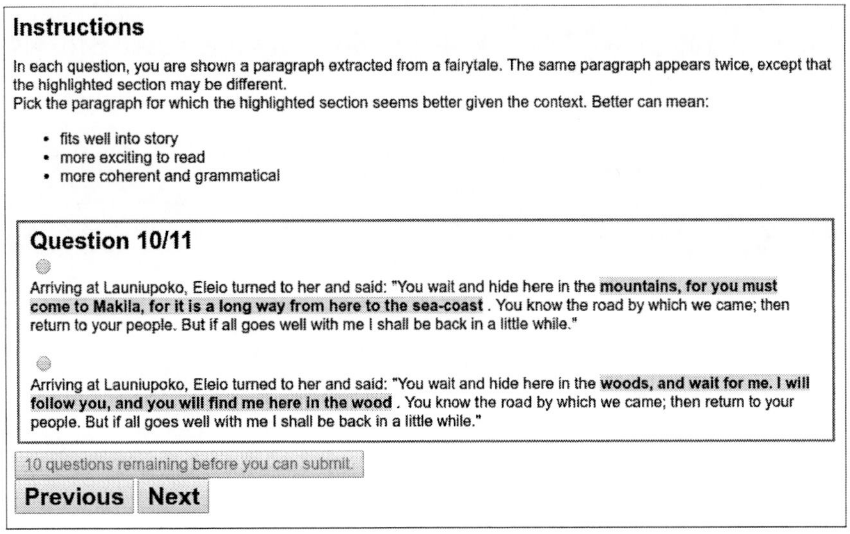

Figure 2: User interface for Amazon Mechanical Turk task.


```
    "optimizer_adam_epsilon": 1e-09,
    "pos": "emb",
    "self_attention_type": "dot_product",
    "train_steps": 1000000,
}
```

Identifying Sensible Lexical Relations in Generated Stories

Melissa Roemmele
SDL Research
mroemmele@sdl.com

Abstract

As with many text generation tasks, the focus of recent progress on story generation has been in producing texts that are perceived to "make sense" as a whole. There are few automated metrics that address this dimension of story quality even on a shallow lexical level. To initiate investigation into such metrics, we apply a simple approach to identifying word relations that contribute to the 'narrative sense' of a story. We use this approach to comparatively analyze the output of a few notable story generation systems in terms of these relations. We characterize differences in the distributions of relations according to their strength within each story.

1 Introduction

Current text generation systems are frequently able to produce output that is linguistically well-formed with regard to sentence-level syntactic and lexical dependencies. Still, when people perceive the generated text as a whole, it often doesn't appear to "make sense". There are many dimensions to what qualifies a text as sensible. Recent work has focused on trying to model commonsense knowledge and reasoning via the domain of narrative. From the perspective of this work, stories encode the rich set of coherence relations between entities and events by which people interpret their experiences. This has led to frameworks that evaluate automated commonsense reasoning through story modeling tasks like predicting what happens next in a story (Mostafazadeh et al., 2016). Accordingly, the challenge of story generation systems is to express the same commonsense relations that establish the coherence of human-authored stories. One barrier to addressing this challenge is how to quantify the presence of these relations in a text. People can readily provide intuitive judgments about whether a story makes sense, but there has been little exploration of cues for these judgments that can be modeled by current NLP analyses, even relatively shallow ones. We address this in this work by examining a simple approach to detecting lexical relations that contribute to the coherence (or what we call 'narrative sense') of a story. We apply this approach to compare the output of a few different story generation systems according to these relations.

Evaluation in general is an ongoing challenge in text generation research, and particularly for open-ended content like stories. Some work has borrowed automated metrics used for evaluation in other generation tasks (e.g. BLEU for machine translation). However, such metrics expect that there is a fixed set of gold standard references to which output should be compared, which is not a fitting assumption for many story generation frameworks. If the task is to generate a story about a particular topic or to generate a story given an opening sentence, there is no finite set of "correct" stories that meet the objective. For this reason, most work relies on human judgment for evaluation (e.g. Fan et al., 2018; Holtzman et al., 2018; Roemmele and Gordon, 2018), often through a quantitative rating or ranking scheme for selected quality dimensions (e.g. asking "how coherent is this story?" or "which story is more coherent?" among a set of candidates). While these judgments are a reliable indicator of the relative impact of different generation models, they are costly in that they must be repeated for each new set of generated output. Moreover, relying on holistic ratings/rankings of quality does not provide insight into the text-level features that influence these judgments. Qualitative feedback is useful for this, but it can be difficult for people to precisely verbalize their intuition about what makes a generated text sound good or bad. Fully modeling this judgment may require sophisticated nat-

Proceedings of the First Workshop on Narrative Understanding, pages 44–52
Minneapolis, Minnesota, June 7, 2019.

ural language understanding capabilities, but we can still investigate whether shallow indicators of this judgment are available.

As more text generation systems are being deployed, comparative evaluations between them are becoming increasingly important. Many researchers have released story generation models trained through their own particular experiments, including those described in Section 2. These already-trained models can be readily used by other NLP practitioners, but re-training them can often require significant time and resources due to their complexity. In some cases (e.g. the GPT-2 system described below), the procedure for training the model is not publicly available. Still, this does not mean any comparative evaluation between systems trained on different datasets is fruitless. Such evaluations may not be able to completely disentangle the contribution of a particular algorithmic approach versus that of the dataset itself, but they can still illuminate the relative impact of each model in the stories it produces. Moreover, they can also help scrutinize any qualitative claims made about the performance of a particular system, since sometimes such claims are based on a handful of carefully selected examples. Our vision is to move towards frameworks that can analyze the characteristics of story generation models even when they are presented as black boxes, simply by observing the stories they generate.

In this work, we analyze stories in terms of word relations in order to investigate whether such relations can be examined as an indicator of narrative sense. As outlined in Section 3, to capture word relations we use a generic NLP technique of calculating statistical word co-occurences in a corpus of stories, in particular by using the Pointwise Mutual Information (PMI) (Church and Hanks, 1990) statistic. The use of statistical word association measures in narrative modeling tasks is familiar. There is work on using these measures to evaluate coherence in news stories (Shahaf and Guestrin, 2010). Other work has used word co-occurrence statistics to predict commonsense cause-effect relations between sentences (Gordon et al., 2011; Luo et al., 2016; Riaz and Girju, 2013; Sasaki et al., 2017). A related line of research has focused on modeling pairs of verb-argument units in narrative text in order to induce story event sequences (Chambers and Jurafsky, 2008; McIntyre and Lapata, 2009; Rudinger et al., 2015). Other relevant tasks like emotional framing of narrative (Jurafsky et al., 2014), sentence completion based on reading comprehension (Woods, 2016), and creative language generation (Toivanen et al., 2014) have also been addressed using lexical association measures. Most relevant to generation evaluation, Sagarkar et al. (2018) demonstrated that quality ratings of generated stories correlated significantly with the average PMI score of their component word pairs found in a story corpus. Our work takes a look at the distribution of word pair PMI scores in stories generated by alternative approaches that have not yet been directly compared.

2 Generation Task

We examined four models that have specifically been applied to story generation and which generate stories based on a seed input text. We used 15,138 items from the test set of the English-language Reddit WritingPrompts dataset[1] (Fan et al., 2018) as these seed inputs. This dataset is derived from the /r/WritingPrompts subreddit, where users write and share fiction stories in response to a story premise (the prompt). Each item in this dataset consists of a prompt and a human-authored story. For each prompt, we generated a story with each of the models described below. We did not train our own version of these models but instead used the already-trained models provided by the respective authors on their linked GitHub repositories.

CREATIVEHELP[2] (Roemmele and Gordon, 2018): An RNN language model trained on a subset of 11,000 self-published fiction books in the Toronto BookCorpus[3].

GPT-2[4] (Radford et al., 2019): A transformer-based language model trained on several million webpages in the WebText corpus. The full model advertised in the paper is not publicly available, so we used the 'small' version of the model. While GPT-2 has been presented as a generic text generation system as opposed to one specifically for story generation, the examples presented by the authors include narrative text.

HIERARCHICAL[5] (Fan et al., 2018): A convolutional sequence-to-sequence model with self-

[1] See github.com/pytorch/fairseq for link to dataset

[2] github.com/roemmele/narrative-prediction

[3] yknzhu.wixsite.com/mbweb

[4] github.com/openai/gpt-2

[5] github.com/pytorch/fairseq

Prompt
On your way to Mars on the first voyage ever , you discover that you and the countless others on the ship are intended ritual sacrifices by Elon Musk . You now must avoid reaching Mars at all costs .

CREATIVEHELP	Your all - sister , state - and - seek , is exactly what you believed was William , WP thought , and agreed with the program . Elon Musk and Jett moved into their strong chamber . At the group of Ryan over from Tumblr , the third was fallen and a wise top dancer and a united East Africans . Here was a light , and I felt really fear or make out William . My heart leapt to my throat ; I 'd trapped Riley in no life between her But Anna was afraid . The real baby boy was doing something for me had led me out of his room . From the fire , it closed and connected with him . Elon Musk looked down at her hands and said , " not just you ! " She looked at me , then shrugged and
GPT-2	But if they can , do so . On Your Way To Mars on the first voyage ever , you discover that you and the countless others on the ship are intended ritual sacrifices by Elon Musk . You now must avoid reaching Mars at all costs . But if they can , do so . Borough of Babel : On your way to Pluto The planet currently inhabited by Jekyllands Islet and its looters bears benefit isty , albeit unable to argue that it is indeed inhabited . Or itself is ; consider the inhabitants of Copernicus themselves , as walking amongst them , does so represent the rarity of the copernican planet , which is understandably deplored . 343.FIRE Required Strange preview gained ID of Wurmby , and 25705 Heat up Any an important bounty hunter might pursue , the real tyrant looks like Javian 's gaze .
HIERARCHICAL	" I am an old man , old man. " " You are the last human to be here , you are the one who will never find us ! " " But I have been the one to bring you the one who will never come back ! " A long pause followed as a young man in a suit and helmet stepped in front of a large screen . " I am not a human man , but I am a man . I am the last human . I am the only human who can not be found . I have been the last human to be taken , you will become the last human . I am the only human . I have been the last human , and every human has been given to me . I am the last human
L2W	it is your duty to make sure that you are safe . " the two men exchanged a long look , then nodded and left . as the door closed behind them , the door swung shut behind them . the room was silent . the room was empty . the room was silent except for the sound of heavy breathing . the room was filled with the sounds of shuffling and shuffling . the room was pitch black and pitch black . the walls and floor of the room were strewn with debris and debris . the room seemed to be suspended above the floor . there were no lights in the room . no sign of anyone else . no one was in sight . there were only two chairs . one of them was a desk . a small desk . a desk sat on the floor
HUMAN	I hid under the tiny bed of my room , terrified . I covered my mouth , trying to muffle my heavy breathing . I heard its footsteps in the distance , dragging it 's feet as it walked . I heard it sniff the air , grunting , as it caught on to a scent . It started walking in a different direction , before suddenly breaking out into a sprint . I gasped instinctively , before realizing it was moving away from me . I lay there , in complete darkness , filled with fear . It had broken the main generators , and the backups only provided power to the main hallways . In the distance , I heard a faint scream , which was soon replaced by a deafening silence . I slowly moved out from under my bed . My hands were trembling , tears

Table 1: Example of a story generated by each model for a given prompt

attention on the decoder. The approach also uses a fusion mechanism that further encourages conditioning on the input while generating. This model was trained on the Reddit WritingPrompts dataset, which is the same dataset we use to seed generation in our work (we use the test set that was not observed by this model during training).

L2W[6] (Holtzman et al., 2018): An RNN language model enhanced with discriminator mechanisms that promote non-repetition, semantic entailment between sentences, relevance, and lexical diversity in the generated output. As with CREATIVEHELP, this model was trained on the BookCorpus stories.

One detail to note is that among these models, only the HIERARCHICAL model is specifically trained to observe the prompt as text that is independent from the generated story itself. The other models are designed for 'story continuation', i.e. generating the next segment of an initial story. Here, these models viewed the prompt as the initial sequence in the story which is continued by the generated text. However, we subsequently disregard the prompt in our analysis and instead focus only on the relations within the generated text itself. These intra-story relations can still be compared across models without consideration of their relevance to the input texts.

Our analysis requires that the generated stories be comparable in length, so we limited the length of each story to 150 tokens. In some cases, due to the design of each model (e.g. some models complete generation when an end-of-story token is generated), the resulting stories were shorter. There were also instances in which the human-

[6] github.com/ari-holtzman/l2w

authored story was shorter. Consequently, we filtered any set of stories associated with the same prompt where at least one of stories contained fewer than 150 tokens. This resulted in 13,453 stories being included in our analysis. Table 1 shows an example of a prompt and the generated stories for that prompt alongside the corresponding human-authored story (labeled HUMAN).

3 Narrative Sense Relations

In line with the discussion above, we refer to the lexical relations examined in this work as 'narrative sense' relations. By scoring word pairs according to how often they appear in the same story, higher scores will indicate pairs with a stronger relation across different stories, i.e. words for which it makes sense that they would appear in the same story.

Though the inputs we provide to the models come a particular genre of English-language stories (self-published internet fiction), we wanted to examine lexical relations that span across different types of stories. Accordingly, we derived the narrative sense relations from four highly-utilized story corpora described below that (to the best of our knowledge) were not observed by the models during training. Obviously, it is not possible to construct a dataset which has full coverage of all sensible pairs that could appear in a set of generated stories. We selected these four diverse corpora to aim for as broad of coverage as possible without overly biasing the dataset towards pairs contained in the training data for any one of the models.

ROCStories[7] (Mostafazadeh et al., 2016): 97,027 five-sentence narratives authored via crowdsourcing. Authors were specifically asked to write stories in simple English about common everyday scenarios.

Visual Information Storytelling (VIST)[8] (Huang et al., 2016): 50,200 five-sentence stories also authored through crowdsourcing. Authors were prompted to write a story from a sequence of photographs depicting a salient "storyable" event.

CMU Plots[9]: 58,862 book/movie plot summaries extracted from Wikipedia. We truncated each of these summaries to its first 150 tokens, consistent with the length of generated stories.

Children's Book Test[10] (Hill et al., 2016): 98 children's novels authored between 1850 and 1950 and freely available through Project Gutenberg (we used the training set only of the full dataset). We segmented each book into passages of 150 tokens, which resulted in 36,987 passages (we subsequently treated each passage as its own story).

We tokenized all 244,216 stories in these corpora and applied lemmatization to the word tokens[11]. Since our analysis targets content words, we removed punctuation/symbols, numbers, and all words included in an English stopword list. We also removed proper nouns in order to reduce story-specific relations such as entity names. We then established a vocabulary of words occurring in at least five stories. As mentioned above, we calculated the PMI co-occurrence of these words. PMI is calculated for each word pair $(w1, w2)$ based on how often the words appear together relative to their individual frequency:

$$PMI(w1, w2) = \frac{count(w1, w2)}{count(w1) * count(w2)} \quad (1)$$

Here, a co-occurrence between two words was counted any time they appeared in the same story, without regard to their order. There is one exception: when the words occur within the same trigram, they are not counted as a co-occurrence. Our aim in doing this was to minimize relations between words that are phrase-dependent in favor of capturing relations that span across the story. This, in addition to the filtering of stop words and ignoring word order, helps to separate narrative sense relations from words that are related by grammatical dependencies, which is not what we are targeting with this analysis.

Using this methodology, we extracted and computed PMI scores for 7,829,163 word pairs consisting of 23,592 lemmatized words in the given dataset. Scores are computed in log space, as shown in Table 3. The scores in this dataset range from -17.25 to -2.30, with a median of -11.66.

4 Analysis of Generated Stories

For each generated story, we applied the same processing done for the stories in the narrative sense relations dataset, i.e. lemmatizing and removing proper nouns, punctuation/symbols, and

[7] cs.rochester.edu/nlp/rocstories

[8] visionandlanguage.net/VIST

[9] cs.cmu.edu/~ark/personas; cs.cmu.edu/~dbamman/booksummaries.html

[10] fb.ai/babi

[11] Tokenization, POS tagging, lemmatization, and stopword removal was done with spaCy: spacy.io

	CREATIVEHELP	GPT-2	HIERARCHICAL	L2W	HUMAN
1. Total raw words	6943	58966	4942	3173	34401
2. Total recognized words	5008 (72.1%)	18165 (30.8%)	4617 (93.4%)	2937 (92.6%)	17068 (49.6%)
3. Mean stories per word	108.51	32.85	62.56	96.95	34.38
4. Mean words	40.39	44.35	21.46	21.17	43.62
5. Mean word pairs	832.26	1283.79	254.54	225.42	1159.00
6. Mean seen word pairs	790.59 (95.2%)	980.85 (77.1%)	242.33 (96%)	217.88 (97%)	937.72 (82.3%)

Table 2: Statistics for the number of unique words and word pairs across all 13,453 evaluated stories

stopwords. Each story is represented as a set of unique words (disregarding their frequencies), and all pairwise combinations between these words are considered in the analyses.

4.1 Word Statistics

Table 2 contains some descriptive statistics for the generated words/pairs according to each model. Note that the term 'word' in this table refers to a unique word type, since all token frequency information is disregarded. Not surprisingly, there are words in the generated stories that are not contained in the vocabulary for the narrative sense relations dataset. Line 1 reports the total number of unique words in each set of stories after filtering/lemmatization (raw words), while Line 2 shows the proportion of these words that also appear in the vocabulary for the narrative sense relations dataset (recognized words). There are many unrecognized words in the GPT-2 and HUMAN stories, but these stories also contain many more recognized words as well (and it should be considered that several of the unrecognized words occur very rarely in these stories, which is not conveyed in the table). With having smaller word sets, the majority of the words in the HIERARCHICAL and L2W stories are recognized. All subsequent lines in the table pertain to the recognized words. Line 3 reports the mean number of stories that each word generated by that model appears in. This is an indication of lexical diversity, where higher numbers indicate higher redundancy of words across stories generated by that model. For example, each of the 4,617 words among HIERARCHICAL stories occurs in 62.56 HIERARCHICAL stories on average. Consistent with the GPT-2 and HUMAN stories featuring a much broader set of words, these stories are much more diversified in their word selection. The CREATIVEHELP and L2W stories have more words that appear redundantly across stories, with less redundancy in the HIERARCHICAL stories. Line 4 reports the mean number of unique words per story. The CREATIVEHELP, GPT-2, and HUMAN stories have far more unique words than the HIERARCHICAL and L2W stories. This finding is qualitatively reflected in Table 1, where the examples for the latter models contain many repeated words. Lines 5 and 6 show the mean number of unique word pairs per story (where both words are recognized) and the proportion of these that also show up in the narrative sense relations dataset. Naturally, there are fewer word pairs for the HIERARCHICAL and L2W stories given that they contain fewer words overall. There is more coverage for these word pairs in the narrative sense relations dataset. Most of the CREATIVEHELP pairs are also recognized from this dataset. In contrast, the GPT-2 and HUMAN stories contain several word pairs that have not been observed in this dataset.

4.2 Distribution of Word Relations

We examined the word pairs for each model according to their PMI scores in the narrative sense relations dataset. All unseen word pairs were assigned the lowest score of the pairs in the dataset (-17.25). Table 3 illustrates the top 10 word pairs with the highest PMI in each of the stories from Table 1.

Figure 1 plots the binned distribution (binned using the Freedman-Diaconis rule (Freedman and Diaconis, 1981)) of PMI scores for all word pairs in the generated stories for each model. The y-axis represents the total number of word pairs with scores in the corresponding bin. The blue area of the graph includes all pairs, while the orange area represents the distribution when only the 100 highest-scoring pairs in each story are considered. The median of each distribution is indicated by the lines of the corresponding color. The plots convey some of the information in Table 2, particularly with regard to the HIERARCHICAL and L2W models generating fewer unique words and thus fewer pairs overall. These particular models also have a much more narrow score distribution, and a higher median score overall relative to the

CREATIVEHELP	GPT-2	HIERARCHICAL	L2W	HUMAN
((chamber, leapt), -9.26)	((ship, voyage), -9.0)	((pause, step), -10.92)	((chair, shuffling), -9.04)	((scent, sniff), -8.59)
((afraid, fear), -10.47)	((inhabitant, planet), -9.29)	((pause, suit), -11.3)	((pitch, swing), -9.66)	((generator, power), -8.97)
(('d, shrug), -10.57)	((inhabit, inhabitant), -9.51)	((follow, human), -11.52)	((breathing, sound), -10.22)	((instinctively, silence), -9.45)
((chamber, throat), -10.59)	((bounty, planet), -9.55)	((come, pause), -11.55)	((silent, strew), -10.24)	((gasp, grunt), -9.53)
(('d, say), -10.65)	((inhabit, ritual), -9.68)	((helmet, man), -11.67)	((floor, strew), -10.27)	((faint, instinctively), -9.54)
((leapt, seek), -10.75)	((planet, ship), -9.69)	((old, young), -11.68)	((chair, sit), -10.47)	((mouth, muffle), -9.62)
((believe, united), -10.78)	((tyrant, voyage), -9.82)	((follow, young), -11.71)	((nod, pitch), -10.61)	((faint, scent), -9.75)
((chamber, room), -10.79)	((inhabitant, tyrant), -10.04)	((pause, screen), -11.71)	((debris, floor), -10.63)	((breathing, darkness), -9.75)
((shrug, strong), -10.83)	((consider, preview), -10.1)	((follow, man), -11.85)	((nod, shut), -10.69)	((direction, scent), -9.89)
((chamber, heart), -10.84)	((sacrifice, tyrant), -10.21)	((human, large), -11.86)	((breathing, safe), -10.72)	((faint, tremble), -9.92)

Table 3: Highest-scoring word pairs for each story from the example in Table 1

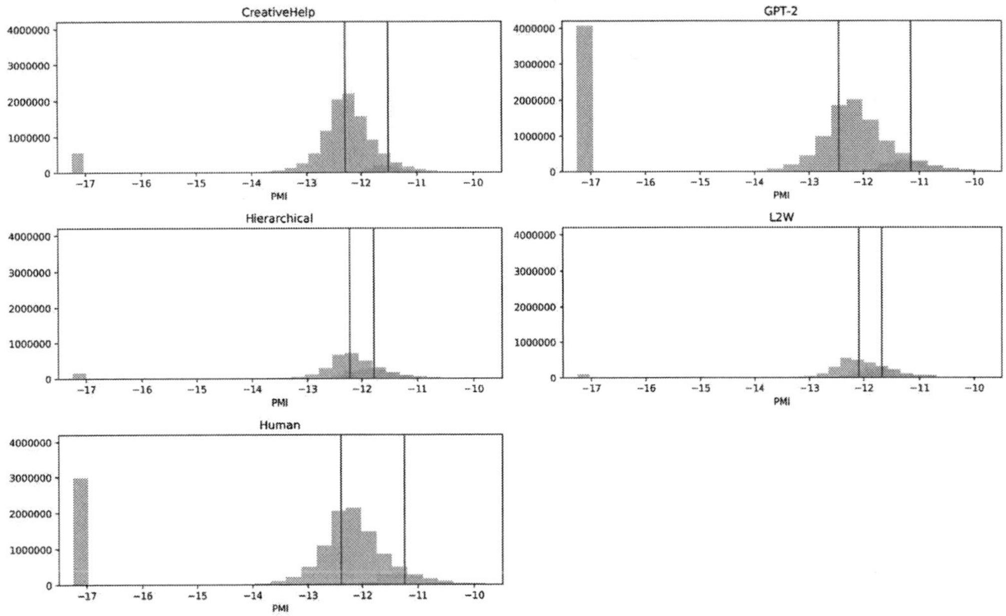

Figure 1: Distribution of word pair scores in generated stories for each model

other models. In contrast, the scores of the CREATIVEHELP, GPT-2, and HUMAN pairs are distributed across a wider range. The large number of pairs not observed in the narrative sense relations datasets for the GPT-2 and HUMAN stories is represented by the tall blue bar on the far left side of each of these plots (since the score of these pairs is set to the lowest PMI score in the narrative sense relations dataset). This causes the median of the full distribution for these models to be much lower. However, these stories also have many more pairs with higher PMI scores, signified by the large gap between the full distribution and the top-100 distribution, where the medians of the latter are much higher for these models. Thus, we can summarize that the HIERARCHICAL and L2W models tend to consistently generate moderately strong relations, but the GPT-2 and HUMAN stories are more likely to contain very strong lexical relations. Interestingly, the median score of the GPT-2 pairs among the top-100 distribution (-11.15) is actually slightly higher than the corresponding HUMAN median (-11.24).

4.3 Distinguishing Narrative Sense Relations

Figure 1 reveals differences in the distribution of lexical relation scores for each model, but the discrepancies in their individual word distributions make it difficult to draw conclusions about how much narrative sense is produced by each model. To try to further interpret the differences between the models, we designed a prediction task that tests whether the lexical relations in each story can be distinguished from spurious relations. In particular, for each generated story represented as a set of words, we artificially created a new story with the same number of words, where the words were randomly sampled from the set of all stories

CREATIVEHELP	GPT-2	HIERARCHICAL	L2W	HUMAN
5571 (41.4%)	6574 (48.9%)	6661 (49.5%)	6104 (45.4%)	7355 (54.7%)

Table 4: Total number of stories (among 13,453) exceeding narrative sense threshold for each model

generated by the corresponding model. Thus, the scores of any relations that emerge in these samples are accounted for by overall word frequency alone. Another way to think about this test is that it determines how easy it is to distinguish relations that occur within a given story to those that occur across different stories. We compared the distribution of scores for the original story to the distribution for the random story using the Wilcoxon rank-sum statistic (Wilcoxon, 1945), which evaluates the difference between two distributions. If this test indicated the original word pair scores were on average higher than the random scores (at a level of statistical significance $p < 0.10$), we assigned the original story a point indicating it exceeded the narrative sense threshold. Exceeding this threshold signifies confidence that the lexical relations between the words in the story 'make sense'. In this scheme, stories with high narrative sense should contain much higher scoring word pairs than would be expected to appear from random combinations of the same words. If there are never differences between these distributions, it suggests that the generated word relations occur largely by chance. Thus, stories with more distinct narrative sense relations should more often exceed the narrative sense threshold.

Table 4 shows the results of this analysis. Note that the narrative sense threshold is quite conservative due to the requirement that the difference between the original and random pairs be statistically significant. Thus, the absolute number of stories that exceed the threshold is low for all models, but we are only concerned with their relative difference. The CREATIVEHELP stories have the least distinct narrative sense relations, which is notable given that their median word pair score is higher than that of the HIERARCHICAL and L2W stories. This suggests many of the relations generated by CREATIVEHELP appear simply due to the number of combinations of words in these stories (since more combinations yields more opportunities to find high-scoring relations in the narrative sense relations dataset). As expected, the HUMAN stories exceed the narrative sense threshold the most often, meaning that their lexical relations are the least likely to be predicted by just the overall frequency of their words. This result also distinguishes the HUMAN stories from the GPT-2 stories, which otherwise show similar score distributions in Figure 1. While the GPT-2 model produces many strong narrative sense relations overall, from the result in Table 4 we can conclude that a single GPT-2 story tends to have less narrative sense than a HUMAN story when their respective overall word distributions are taken into account. Moreover, the HIERARCHICAL stories also demonstrate stronger narrative sense relations than the GPT-2 stories according to this analysis, even though the former produces fewer high-scoring pairs overall.

5 Conclusion

We demonstrated an analysis of lexical relations in generated stories with an emphasis on identifying 'narrative sense' relations that contribute to perceived story coherence. This work is intended to support the development of automated metrics that detect whether a generated text is sensible, in order to reduce the expense of exclusively relying on human judgment for this type of evaluation. We extracted word relations in the generated output of four published story generation systems that have not previously been compared on the same set of story inputs. We discovered interesting differences in the relations produced by each model, and presented a way to characterize these relations according to how well they can be discriminated from relations that appear by chance. These results indicate that the human-authored stories feature strong narrative sense relations that distinguish them from the generated stories. Differences among the generated models are also apparent. As future work, we can reproduce this analysis using a different narrative sense relations dataset to better determine the impact of this dataset on exposing these differences.

In this work, the narrative sense of a lexical relation is vouched for by its repeated appearance in other stories, so the focus is on rewarding models for producing these relations. An alternative analysis could instead look for relations that violate some aspect of commonsense knowledge. This would shift the focus of the analysis to penalizing models for producing relations that detract from the coherence of the story. However, it is also important to point out that an ideal story generation system would model human creativity in producing content that has not been observed in any existing story. Presumably many of the previously unseen pairs appearing in the human-authored stories are reflective of this creativity while also not necessarily violating commonsense. Future work should examine how to evaluate the capacity of systems to induce novel lexical relations that support story coherence.

References

Nathanael Chambers and Dan Jurafsky. 2008. Unsupervised learning of narrative event chains. In *46th Annual Meeting of the Association of Computational Linguistics*, pages 789–797.

Kenneth Ward Church and Patrick Hanks. 1990. Word association norms, mutual information, and lexicography. *Computational linguistics*, 16(1):22–29.

Angela Fan, Mike Lewis, and Yann Dauphin. 2018. Hierarchical neural story generation. In *Proceedings of the 56th Annual Meeting of the Association for Computational Linguistics (Volume 1: Long Papers)*, volume 1, pages 889–898.

David Freedman and Persi Diaconis. 1981. On the histogram as a density estimator: L 2 theory. *Probability theory and related fields*, 57(4):453–476.

Andrew Gordon, Cosmin Adrian Bejan, and Kenji Sagae. 2011. Commonsense Causal Reasoning Using Millions of Personal Stories. *Twenty-Fifth Conference on Artificial Intelligence (AAAI-11)*, pages 1180–1185.

F. Hill, A. Bordes, S. Chopra, and J. Weston. 2016. The goldilocks principle: Reading children's books with explicit memory representations. In *International Conference on Learning Representations*.

Ari Holtzman, Jan Buys, Maxwell Forbes, Antoine Bosselut, David Golub, and Yejin Choi. 2018. Learning to write with cooperative discriminators. In *Proceedings of the Association for Computational Linguistics*.

Ting-Hao K. Huang, Francis Ferraro, Nasrin Mostafazadeh, Ishan Misra, Jacob Devlin, Aishwarya Agrawal, Ross Girshick, Xiaodong He, Pushmeet Kohli, Dhruv Batra, et al. 2016. Visual storytelling. In *15th Annual Conference of the North American Chapter of the Association for Computational Linguistics (NAACL 2016)*.

Dan Jurafsky, Victor Chahuneau, Bryan Routledge, and Noah Smith. 2014. Narrative framing of consumer sentiment in online restaurant reviews. *First Monday*, 19(4).

Zhiyi Luo, Yuchen Sha, Kenny Q. Zhu, Seung-won Hwang, and Zhongyuan Wang. 2016. Commonsense causal reasoning between short texts. In *15th International Conference on Principles of Knowledge Representation and Reasoning (KR-2016)*.

Neil McIntyre and Mirella Lapata. 2009. Learning to tell tales: A data-driven approach to story generation. In *Proceedings of the Joint Conference of the 47th Annual Meeting of the ACL and the 4th International Joint Conference on Natural Language Processing of the AFNLP*, pages 217–225, Stroudsburg, PA, USA. Association for Computational Linguistics.

Nasrin Mostafazadeh, Nathanael Chambers, Xiaodong He, Devi Parikh, Dhruv Batra, Lucy Vanderwende, Pushmeet Kohli, and James Allen. 2016. A corpus and cloze evaluation for deeper understanding of commonsense stories. In *Proceedings of NAACL-HLT*, pages 839–849.

Alec Radford, Jeff Wu, Rewon Child, David Luan, Dario Amodei, and Ilya Sutskever. 2019. Language models are unsupervised multitask learners.

Mehwish Riaz and Roxana Girju. 2013. Toward a better understanding of causality between verbal events: Extraction and analysis of the causal power of verb-verb associations. In *Proceedings of the SIGDIAL 2013 Conference*, pages 21–30, Metz, France. Association for Computational Linguistics.

Melissa Roemmele and Andrew S Gordon. 2018. Automated assistance for creative writing with an rnn language model. In *Proceedings of the 23rd International Conference on Intelligent User Interfaces Companion*, page 21. ACM.

Rachel Rudinger, Pushpendre Rastogi, Francis Ferraro, and Benjamin Van Durme. 2015. Script induction as language modeling. In *Proceedings of the 2015 Conference on Empirical Methods in Natural Language Processing*. Association for Computational Linguistics.

Manasvi Sagarkar, John Wieting, Lifu Tu, and Kevin Gimpel. 2018. Quality signals in generated stories. In *Proceedings of the Seventh Joint Conference on Lexical and Computational Semantics*, pages 192–202. Association for Computational Linguistics.

Shota Sasaki, Sho Takase, Naoya Inoue, Naoaki Okazaki, and Kentaro Inui. 2017. Handling multiword expressions in causality estimation. In *IWCS 201712th International Conference on Computational SemanticsShort papers*.

Dafna Shahaf and Carlos Guestrin. 2010. Connecting the dots between news articles. In *Proceedings of the 16th ACM SIGKDD International Conference on*

Knowledge Discovery and Data Mining, KDD '10, pages 623–632, New York, NY, USA. ACM.

Jukka Toivanen, Oskar Gross, and Hannu Toivonen. 2014. The officer is taller than you, who race yourself! using document specific word associations in poetry generation.

Frank Wilcoxon. 1945. Individual comparisons by ranking methods. *Biometrics bulletin*, 1(6):80–83.

Aubrie Woods. 2016. Exploiting linguistic features for sentence completion. In *Proceedings of the 54th Annual Meeting of the Association for Computational Linguistics (Volume 2: Short Papers)*, pages 438–442, Berlin, Germany. Association for Computational Linguistics.

Author Index

Association for Computational Linguistics
209 N. Eighth Street
Stroudsburg, Pennsylvania 18360

ISBN 978-1-5108-8778-7

CURRAN ASSOCIATES INC.
proceedings.com